THE UNCONSCIOUS EDGE

The Five-Step Framework to Transform Your Thinking and Unlock Your True Potential

DONALD HAMILTON

**The Unconcious Edge:
The Five-Step Framework to Transform Your Thinking and Unlock Your True Potential**
© 2025 Donald Hamilton LLP

All rights reserved. No part of this book may be reproduced, stored in a retrieval system or transmitted in any form or by any means (electronic, mechanical, photocopy, recording, scanning or other) except for brief quotations in critical reviews or articles, without the prior written permission of the publisher.

ISBN: 9781068460029 Paperback

Published by: Inspired By Publishing

The strategies in this book are presented primarily for enjoyment and educational purposes. Every effort has been made to trace copyright holders and obtain their permission for the use of copyright material.

Disclaimer

The information, techniques and audio files presented in this book and/or through the qr codes contained in it are intended for educational and informational purposes to help enable a mindset for success only.

They are not intended as therapy for any mental health condition nor as a substitute for professional medical or psychological advice, diagnosis or treatment.

The reader uses them at their own risk.

Hypnosis is a safe and low-risk activity for most individuals when practised correctly. However, hypnosis may not be suitable for everyone. Please read and follow the health warning in Appendix 2 before deciding whether to use any hypnosis audio in, or linked to this book.

The author and publisher disclaim any liability for any direct or indirect consequences arising from the use or application of the information and/or the hypnosis audios contained in and/or linked to from this book.

Acknowledgements

In writing this book, I have truly stood on the shoulders of giants. These are the people who have helped shape me, my practice, my knowledge, my skills and my expertise, and I would like to recognise some of them now.

First, I want to acknowledge the late R. Paul Russell, my first boss and colleague at Accenture. Many years ago, when I was at a crossroads in my life and career, Paul showed absolute trust and faith in me. Without his support, I cannot say where I would be today, but I am certain I would not have had the career, the life and the success that I have enjoyed.

Running only marginally second to Paul is my friend, mentor and client Steve Bolton. We are opposites that complement each other perfectly; Steve hates doing the things that I do, and I can only look on in awe at Steve's big-picture thinking and boundless enthusiasm. Whenever I am unsure where to turn or what to do, Steve has always stepped in with wise guidance or great opportunities. I was absolutely delighted when he agreed to write the Foreword to this book.

When it comes to negotiation – understanding both the process and the personal dynamics involved, as well as learning how to teach these concepts in an engaging and enjoyable way – I couldn't have asked for better guidance and support than from my friends, colleagues and partners at CMI Concord, Paul Cramer and, especially, Chuck Barker. I am truly in their debt. I extend my sincere thanks to Chuck for reviewing the manuscript and kindly granting permission to use certain graphics in Chapters 8 and 9.

In the fields of Coaching, NLP and Hypnotherapy, I have been fortunate to work with and learn from some of the best in the business – Ali Campbell, Freddy and Anthony Jacquin of the Jacquin Hypnosis Academy and, in the field of corporate hypnotism, the late Anthony Galie, who sadly passed away as I was in the process of writing this book. All have given their time freely and unstintingly, and they continue to do so as I pursue the never-ending journey towards becoming an outstanding hypnotherapist and coach. Many of the techniques I have described in the book or used in the hypnosis audios were learned from these masters of the art!

I am also deeply grateful to Inspired By Publishing for the opportunity to write this book – especially to Angela Haynes-Ranger, who took on the task of managing me through the writing process. With patience and perseverance, she kept me (more or less) on track, despite setbacks and my own moments of procrastination as I questioned whether I could truly write a book!

Finally, and most importantly, there are no words to express my gratitude for the support and patience I have received from my family – my wife, Christine, and my sons, Ally and Dougie. They have always supported all my ventures and flights of fancy, however crazy they seem. Love you guys!

Foreword

When it comes to versatility, professionalism and the ability to inspire, Donald stands out as one of the most remarkable individuals I've had the privilege to work with in over 40 years of business.

I first met Donald in 2010, shortly after his return from a year-long trip around the world with his wife and two young sons. This journey followed a distinguished 16-year career at Accenture, a Fortune 100 company, where he held several senior legal positions and served as a faculty member at their Negotiation Centre of Excellence. At that time, Donald was beginning a new chapter, transitioning into a portfolio career that included launching his own commercial and negotiation consultancy. Simultaneously, he was exploring an investment in a property franchise business where I served as CEO.

Donald's enthusiasm for learning and teaching, coupled with his sharp intellect and sense of humour, immediately drew me in. Recognising his talent, I invited him to deliver a negotiation training session at one of our quarterly franchisee workshops. His session was nothing short of extraordinary – engaging, interactive and genuinely transformative for the 120 attendees. The feedback was phenomenal, setting a benchmark for the workshops we hosted.

Shortly after, we encountered a challenging negotiation with a potential board appointee that had reached an impasse. Emotions were high, and progress seemed impossible. I reached out to Donald for advice. Over an hour-long conversation, he reframed the situation entirely, providing practical, non-confrontational steps to resolve the conflict. His guidance not only helped us achieve a fair and mutually beneficial outcome but also reshaped my approach to negotiation. His principles have served me well ever since. Since then, Donald has been an integral part of every business I've built – sometimes in an advisory capacity, other times as a coach, and often as both. In my current venture, Bolt Angels, he has been recognised as "Advisor of the Year" for two years running, a testament to the consistent value he brings.

Throughout his career, Donald has demonstrated an unparalleled ability to adapt and excel. His ventures into hypnotherapy and NLP were natural extensions of his lifelong curiosity about what drives human behaviour. Whether helping individuals overcome limiting beliefs or delivering executive mindset training, Donald's work has been transformative, with results that have positively impacted both personal and professional lives.

It's no surprise that Donald has finally written this book. For years, I and many others have encouraged him to share his insights and methods with a wider audience. The timing couldn't be better. In a world increasingly concerned with mindset and mental health, this book is a guide to understanding how our beliefs and patterns are formed and, more importantly, how we can reshape them to achieve success.

When I think about Donald's multifaceted talents, one example comes to mind. At a Bolt Angels AGM and social event that I attended, he seamlessly moved between updating the team on a complex negotiation, delivering a comedy hypnosis performance that left the audience in stitches and securing a new client to deliver executive training. That same week, he had conducted coaching sessions across three continents in a single day – an audience in South Africa at 6am, a mutual client in London mid-day, and another group in Europe at 9pm. Donald's energy, expertise and relentless commitment to making a difference never cease to amaze me.

This book encapsulates all that makes Donald exceptional. It is not just a manual for overcoming limiting beliefs – it is a blueprint for transformation. Read it, absorb its lessons and take action. I'm confident the results will speak for themselves.

Steve Bolton

Steve Bolton is a serial entrepreneur and, with his current venture Bolt Angels, has become a visionary leader in the angel investment world – known for combining entrepreneurial expertise with a passion for innovation and a distinctive investment philosophy. You can read his full, fascinating life story at www.stevebolton.com.

Contents

Introduction	1
Chapter 1 - Milton Keynes Changed My Life	5
Chapter 2 - How Your Mind Works (Or Why You Believed in Santa Claus)	15
Chapter 3 - The ASDIC Framework	35
Chapter 4 - Acceptance	49
Chapter 5 - Stabilisation	59
Chapter 6 - Development	81
Chapter 7 - Improvement	105
Chapter 8 - Consistency	133
Chapter 9 - Bonus Chapter: Introduction to Negotiation	155
Chapter 10 - Closing Thoughts: Adding Experience & Skill to Knowledge	177
Appendix 1: Conditions Matrix	181
Appendix 2: Hypnosis Health Warning	184
Resources	185
References	188
About the Author	190

Introduction

"A journey of a thousand miles begins with a single step."
– Chinese proverb

Have you ever watched a successful person, whether in business, sport or any other field and wondered, "How do they do that?" or "What do they have in themselves that allows them to get to that level and make it look so effortless?" These thoughts are often quickly followed by "What do I need to do to be like that?" or, in many cases, "I don't think I could do that" or "I don't think I've got it in me to do that."

There is no doubt that the most successful people have a mindset that drives success. For starters, it may have one or several components – drive, focus, vision, confidence, self-belief, leadership and effective communication. Some may be instinctive, but most will have been "learned" wittingly or unwittingly over time. The common element is that they have adopted them in such a way that they no longer think about them consciously. While there may be disciplines or approaches that they apply consciously – how they prepare for a specific meeting, how they approach a specific task, how they will interact with a particular audience, for example – they have adopted the core elements that make them successful so that they are automatic. They are just part of "who they are", and they no longer need to think about them. These are the unconscious aspects of success – the elements that give them an "Unconscious Edge."

But how do you achieve this mindset and develop and empower your teams to do the same?

If you find yourself asking these questions, then this book is for you. It is for anyone who aspires to be successful but struggles to develop the right mindset or move forward with confidence. It is for the (many) people who have developed the "unconscious aspects of not quite making it" – perhaps because they feel something in them is holding them back. Maybe they are riven with self-doubt about their decision-making, feel they are not good enough or lack the necessary skills and ability, believe they don't deserve to be there or are simply afraid of failure. The list of things that you may feel are holding you back is long!

In my hypnotherapy and coaching practices, I have worked with many executives who struggled that way – I have been one myself, and I know how uncomfortable and frustrating it can feel.

If that's you, the good news is that you are not alone. It is not your fault. You have done nothing wrong and are not a failure. You have been hard-wired that way by your life experiences –

even if you don't remember those experiences! The even better news is that, by tapping into your subconscious and taking a few quick and easy actions, you can do something about it. Change that hardwiring and the way it makes you feel and act, and launch yourself on the path to success. This book introduces a framework – the ASDIC Framework – that contains a number of ways in which you can do that, along with some ninja tips on managing relationships with other people more effectively and obtaining win-win outcomes.

While it may well be self-evident, not everybody starts from the same point. You will often hear people ask, "On a scale of 0 to 10, where are you on your journey to being successful?" or something similar. In my experience, that scale is wrong – or, at least, it only tells half the story. I believe that the true scale is -10 to +10, where 0 is "neutral."

The negative numbers represent the limiting beliefs, patterns and blockers deep in people's subconscious that stop them from even getting to neutral. These include impostor syndrome, anxiety, feeling that they are not good enough or fear of failure. I even know of a lawyer who was so terrified of being "found out" that he would fall ill on the morning of every final contract signing. Unable to face the meeting, he would call in sick – meaning he never actually witnessed the signing of any of the contracts he had worked so hard on. If you find yourself in that zone – and, believe me, many people do (though they rarely admit it for fear of being seen as "weak") – take another look at the good news and the even better news above. You can do something about it!

The starting point is always to work out where a person is on the scale and, if necessary, how to get that person to neutral. Once there, the mental shackles are off, and the focus changes to developing the mindset and skills to achieve peak performance.

The ASDIC Framework is my way of taking you on the journey from that starting point to an endpoint where you are consistently performing at your best without even thinking about it – and enjoying the success that follows. It is intended to be a practical approach based on what I have learned and the experiences I have gained throughout my career.

Change will come from engaging fully in this journey. Believe in the framework and practise the techniques and skills consistently. As you do so, you will find that your confidence, self-belief and engagement will increase, and you will progress on your journey.

For me, that journey and the journey to creating that framework began many years ago in Milton Keynes…

Chapter 1
Milton Keynes Changed My Life

"The mind, once stretched by a new idea, never returns to its original dimensions."
– Ralph Waldo Emerson

My interest in understanding the mental "programmes" that we all run, the subconscious programmes that can either hold us back or take us forward, began in earnest in the late 1990s – at a negotiation training session in Milton Keynes. "Milton Keynes changed my life" is not a phrase that you will hear very often, but it is true for me!

I was an in-house attorney at Accenture, the technology and management consultancy, specialising in negotiating large international outsourcing contracts. I had years of experience in complex negotiations and, frankly, saw this session and the trip to Milton Keynes as a bit of a jolly – I thought that I had seen it all, done it all and knew it all. How wrong I was!

The instructor was a guy called Paul Cramer, who would go on to become a friend and business partner, and he started by doing two exercises. First, he sold one of the attendees a £20 note for £40, which really got my attention. Then, he did the exercise that changed everything for me.

I still do this exercise today in the courses I run – indeed, I can teach my whole executive development course off of it. I am going to walk you through a version of that exercise, so if you think you may ever come to one of my courses or, really, go to any negotiation course, please do not read the next few paragraphs. Just skip them and start reading again where you see the self-explanatory "OK – START READING AGAIN HERE."

Paul started by having everyone sit across the table from another participant, pairing us up.

He then said, "I'll show you what I want you to do," and had his co-presenter sit across from him. They placed their right elbows on the table and clasped hands in the classic arm-wrestling position. He looked at the participants and said, "With your partner, adopt the position." With a few moans and groans, everyone did.

"Starting when I say 'Go,'" he said, "there's only one rule: Every time your partner's hand touches the table, you earn a point." For each point, he offered a £5 reward. Then he called out, "Go!"

Tables were gripped, muscles tensed and sinews strained as participants wrestled their partners' hands down, eager to win both points and pounds.

Eventually, before anyone burst a blood vessel or tore a rotator cuff, Paul said, "Stop." He asked everybody what their goal had been. Some people said "to win," others said "to beat that guy," but most people said "to win as much money as possible."

With great show, Paul then peeled off £5 notes from the stack he was holding and said, "How much do I owe you then?" A few people had won two points, a slight few more had won one point, but, with sheepish looks, most pairs admitted that neither of them had won any points.

"OK," said Paul, "What was your strategy?" Everybody then gave a variation of "Use my strength to overpower them." To this, Paul replied, "Hmmm, given that I am still holding most of the money, it doesn't sound like that worked so well as an approach. Assume the position again and see if you can work out a way to make more money from the exercise." We did note, though, that at that point, Paul said it was now a theoretical exercise and that he would no longer be paying out the cash!

Each pair reset their positions, discussed their strategy, and soon, nearly everyone adopted a back-and-forth motion – like a windscreen wiper – alternately tapping the back of each other's hand on the table. One pair, however, took a different approach. Instead of alternating, they repeatedly tapped their joined hands on the table, all on one side. This kept one participant's hand just a centimetre above the surface before being tapped down again, while the other's hand never touched the table at all.

Paul stopped the exercise again and asked how much everybody had made. Looking proud, each pair who had taken the "windscreen wiper" approach announced greatly increased gains. The pair who repeatedly and rapidly touched one of their hands on the table reported a massive amount.

"Not bad," said Paul. Approaching a pair that used the "windscreen wiper" method, he held their joined hands upright and asked, "How much were you making when your hands were here?"

"Nothing," they replied.

He shifted their hands slightly to one side. "What about here?"

"Nothing."

Paul continued moving their hands to various positions where neither hand touched the table, each time repeating the question, "How much were you making when your hands were here?" And each time, the answer remained the same: "Nothing."

Paul explained, "That's not unusual. You started communicating, and you greatly increased the value you created – but you were a bit wary of losing out to the other person so you, consciously or unconsciously, adopted a 'one for me, one for you' approach, so it felt fair and no one felt cheated."

He then turned his attention to the pair who had continually and rapidly only tapped one of their hands. "How much money did you make?" he asked, and they told him the large amount they had amassed. He then looked at the person whose hand had always touched the table and said, "Well, that's how much your partner made, but how much did you make? It looks to me like you made nothing. Remember, the rule is you only get £5 if his hand touches the table, but his never did."

"He'll share it with me," the participant replied sheepishly. Paul raised an eyebrow. "Did you discuss that? Did you agree on sharing – or how you'd split it?"

"No," the participant admitted, grinning. "But I trust him… and I know where he lives." Laughter erupted around the room.

Paul stepped back and asked the group, "Do you see the progression? When you treated it as a competition, a battle, and tried to overpower each other, you were both exhausted and generated little or no value. When you started communicating, even when you were wary of each other, you created greater value – and then, when you started to trust each other, you created much more value than you thought possible when you began. So, adopt the position and put your minds to it again – how can you create even more value?" The participants started discussing. Then one pair separated their hands and each started tapping the back of one of their hands on the table – then another pair and another pair. A couple of the more cautious ones asked, "Is it ok to separate our hands?" and Paul repeated, "There is only one rule – when the back of the other person's hand touches the table, you win a point." Everyone joined in soon after that.

As we did this, Paul implored us to think harder – how could we create even more value? We were all now in the zone, and very soon, one pair started tapping the backs of both their hands on the table, doubling the number of points they were earning.

As everyone noticed this and started tapping the backs of both their hands on the table, Paul called a halt and noted that we had added yet another step to the progression. "When you stop treating it as a battle, communicate openly and trust each other, then you create an environment where you can innovate and keep innovating together to create exponential value.

This was already revelatory to me – a lightbulb moment. Then he asked the question that changed everything for me, gave me a full-on floodlight moment (because a lightbulb wasn't nearly bright enough!): "It's great you learned from that exercise and worked through that progression – but why did you arm wrestle in the first place? I didn't say it was arm wrestling, I just said, 'Adopt the position.'"

Stunned silence.

Paul went on to explain that our brains are pattern-recognition devices. We use our life experiences to "learn" patterns. As soon as we recognise (or think we recognise) a pattern, we instantly suspend critical thinking and follow it. This drives almost all of our thoughts and behaviours as humans.

So when he demonstrated the arm wrestling position, everyone's mind recognised a pattern – we have all seen arm wrestling! – and immediately followed it. Our brains were so hardwired that we didn't even think about it, never mind challenging the "rules" of the pattern or the process.

    OK – START READING AGAIN HERE.

Wow! Forget negotiations; this shone a new light on everything. *Our brains are pattern-recognition devices that use our life experiences to "learn" patterns and as soon as they recognise (or think they recognise) a pattern, they instantly suspend critical thinking and follow it. This drives almost all of our thoughts and behaviours as humans.* If our minds are unconsciously following "learned" patterns, running internal programmes if you like, and making us behave in a certain way in certain situations, what effect do they have on other aspects of our lives?

And so began my journey – one that led me to see human behavior in a new light. I started to understand why we learn and follow patterns (which is often beneficial!), how we learn them, and, if we need to, how we can change them. To do this, I studied and became qualified to practise Neuro-Linguistic Programming (NLP) and clinical hypnotherapy.

Neuro-linguistic programming looks at how thoughts (neuro) and words (linguistic) can create these patterns (programming) in our minds. Clinical hypnotherapy is a way to explore the power of the unconscious mind and use it to help ourselves and others overcome challenges and achieve the life we want. It can be used for everything from quitting smoking and conquering phobias to managing IBS, reducing anxiety and achieving peak performance in business and sports.

As my hypnotherapy and NLP practice developed, the overlap between it and my previous life in the corporate world became ever more apparent. I knew the hopes and fears of aspiring executives; I knew the limiting beliefs and self-doubts they held but could not express. I knew that the "functional" skills (however excellent) that got people promoted to executive level were different from the skills required to thrive at that level. And I realised that I was uniquely placed to help them on that journey. Not only did I have the "therapeutic" insights, skills and techniques, but I also knew many of the key practical skills – building relationships, building rapport and effective communication – that helped people succeed

As I worked in these areas, I developed and codified my approach into the ASDIC Framework: Acceptance, Stabilisation, Development, Improvement and Consistency. This is the framework I use in all my sessions with executives, whether in group training sessions, conference speeches or 1:1 coaching.

This book represents the results of my journey so far, and I am delighted that you will be joining me on it. While the ASDIC Framework is my creation, I won't pretend that all the techniques I discuss or use in it are my original thinking. Many are based on or represent well-established principles and approaches, identified and developed by people far smarter than me. But in introducing these to you, in the context of the ASDIC Framework, I believe that I have been truly standing on the shoulders of giants.

Oh, and the answer to the question, "What effect were these subconscious patterns having on other aspects of our lives?" is simple: They control nearly everything we do. In fact, only about 3 to 5% of our daily actions are conscious decisions; the rest are habitual patterns embedded in our subconscious. As you'll discover in the pages ahead, these patterns shape far more than we realise!

Chapter 2
How Your Mind Works (Or Why You Believed in Santa Claus)

> *"Until you make the unconscious conscious, it will direct your life and you will call it fate."*
> – Carl Jung

Yup, as I said at the end of the previous chapter, no more than 5% of what you do every day is done consciously. Everything else – the other 95 to 97% – is done unconsciously, controlled or directed by your unconscious or subconscious mind. (I will use the terms "subconscious" and "unconscious" interchangeably).

You're probably familiar with the idea that we have two parts to our mind – the conscious and the subconscious. But far fewer people truly understand what each one does, why they function the way they do and how large portions of the subconscious are "programmed" to respond automatically to certain situations. This understanding is key to recognising why you react the same way – experiencing the same thoughts, feelings or behaviours – whenever you face the same circumstances. More importantly, it explains why changing these reactions through conscious thought alone is so difficult!

I will look at them as separate parts of your mind, although there is no known physical separation between them. Indeed, there is an ongoing debate about what your mind is as opposed to your brain. I won't open that can of worms in this book!

I have a great interest in this area of study as I believe that in the education system and much of later life, we are only ever taught what to think, not *how* to think. At school, we were rewarded for retaining and reciting facts – very rarely for using our brains creatively.

The Conscious Mind

Your conscious mind is your everyday thinking mind. It is rational, it is logical, it has a limited capacity and it likes linear thinking – proceeding from what it perceives as facts to a logical conclusion. It is based on the here and now. It houses your short-term memory but can really only handle between five and nine things (typically seven) at once. In fact, even that may be overstating it. I recently heard of research that found it could only hold three things at once. As an example, if you're sitting down, notice the pressure of your chair on your back and the backs of your legs – it has always been there, but I bet you didn't even notice it until I drew your attention to it.

The Unconscious Mind

Your unconscious mind does everything else! Its primary function is to keep you safe. It is where your amygdala, responsible for your "fight, flight, freeze" response, sits. If you're unfamiliar with the "fight, flight, freeze" response, it activates when you encounter a situation that you – or your unconscious mind – perceive as dangerous. As soon as the situation arises, your amygdala is instantly alerted and, within a split second, decides whether to flee (flight), confront the threat (fight) or remain completely still (freeze) – sometimes just long enough to assess whether another response might be more effective.

It is often referred to as flight or fight, but freeze is actually the most common response. In the wildlife shows you've watched, I'm sure you've seen zebras suddenly freeze and stand stock still when they suspect a lion may be in the vicinity. During this "frozen" moment, they are deciding whether to stay still and rely on their natural camouflage or run away at full speed. I don't think any of us have ever seen a zebra decide to fight when other options are still available!

Even for humans, this is a primordial response that has served us well since the earliest days. It kept our ancestors safe from sabre-toothed tigers, and we would not be here today without it.

However, the unconscious mind does so much more than just keep us safe: It is creative, intuitive and seemingly endlessly scalable and flexible. It regulates all of your bodily processes, stores and manages your memories, takes learnings from every experience you have ever had (and even some that were only vividly imagined!), files them away and uses those "files" to create the mental patterns and templates that shape your life. It is instinctive and can instantly change the way you think, feel and behave.

For example, imagine you are lying in bed – you're warm, cosy and completely relaxed. Your mind is wandering. Suddenly, you hear a massive bang from the kitchen. In a split second, you're alert and fully focused, the warmth, cosiness and relaxation all forgotten. That's your unconscious mind at work, deciding whether the safest response is to fight, flee or freeze. I'm sure you can think of many other situations in your life where your mood, feelings and behaviours changed in an instant!

The Roles of the Conscious and Unconscious in Everyday Life

In simple terms, you can think about your conscious mind as, for the most part, an observer – an interested and often bemused one – and commentator on your life. It watches events unfold, notes how you feel and act, and occasionally responds with frustration or confusion. So, the conscious part of your mind notices when you feel a bit anxious, out of place in a meeting with senior executives or burdened by a vague sense of inadequacy or an unexplainable fear of failure. Similarly, outside of your professional life, it might register a rising panic at the sight of a spider or while boarding a plane, or notice a sudden craving for a cigarette.

These are things that we notice ourselves every day. However, when you think about it and ask yourself what created the feelings, you will realise that they actually stem from something much deeper. Your conscious mind may have noticed those feelings, but they were created in a different part of your mind – your subconscious.

It's a bit like going on a long road trip with your parents as a child – perhaps on holiday or to visit old Aunt Agatha. Your conscious mind is like the child (the passenger), while your subconscious mind is like the parent driving the car.

The child – your conscious mind – may enjoy the trip, noticing cows in the fields or people in passing buildings, occasionally dipping into their Pick & Mix, but they have no influence over the journey. While they can decide which sweets to eat, they have little control over the destination, the route, the speed or even the choice of music or temperature in the car.

It is the parent – the driver, your subconscious mind – who controls these decisions and determines whether to keep things as they are or change them. It doesn't matter how much the child wants to go somewhere else (not old Aunt Agatha's again!) or take a different route to pass a toy shop or a theme park (or, in my case as a child, a football stadium). Unless they can capture the driver's attention, communicate their point and convince them that their option is better – or at the very least, safe – nothing will change. The journey will continue as it always has.

If, in that analogy, the child wants to make the change, then they must have a way of getting through to, and then communicating effectively with, the parent.

Similarly, if we want to make changes to "the way it has always been" in terms of our thoughts, feelings or behaviours, and the outcomes that we get as a result, we have to have a way of accessing and communicating with our subconscious mind. We will explore a number of ways in which this can be done as we go through the ASDIC Framework.

Now, I'm guessing that, as you are reading this book, you have probably experienced feeling a certain way that you don't particularly like or want to feel but can't seem to shift it, no matter how hard you try. At work, you may have felt anxious, weighed down by impostor syndrome or convinced you're not good enough. In your personal life, you might struggle with cigarette cravings despite knowing the harm smoking causes or experience fear from a phobia you've tried – and failed – to talk yourself out of, fully aware of its irrationality.

If you have a fear of flying and have tried to talk yourself into getting on a plane, then you will know exactly what I mean: Your subconscious raises your stress levels and heart rate, making you feel sick. You really, really don't want to get on that plane! At the same time, your conscious mind knows full well that flying is one of the safest forms of transport, but it's struggling to win the argument with your unconscious mind.

And if you've ever had a strong craving – like for a cigarette – and tried to resist by reminding yourself of its dangers, even the risk of death, you'll know how little influence your conscious mind has over your subconscious. More often than not, you'll end up having that cigarette anyway.

So to summarise: Your conscious mind is, with limited exceptions, the observer, primarily noticing what we are feeling – whether fear, anxiety, cravings and the like – but has very little ability to do anything about it.

The subconscious part is the one constantly asking itself how to make sure you are safe: "What state can I create in their mind and/or body to make sure that they are ok and not exposed to what I, the unconscious, perceive to be danger?" And, of course, if it perceives danger or the chance of hurt, whether physical or emotional, it creates a state of fear, anxiety or something else. At other times, it may create other physical responses – an increased heart rate, a feeling of nausea, perhaps sweating or blushing. It might even create something more extreme, such as a skin disorder like eczema or psoriasis, or even IBS or sudden pain. It will sometimes create a craving or an urge. There is no logic to what it creates to try and fulfil its positive intention – its job is to keep you safe from what it perceives as "dangerous", and it will do anything possible to achieve that.

This is important because, as you follow the chain, your thoughts generate feelings, those feelings drive your actions and behaviours, and those actions and behaviours ultimately determine the outcomes you achieve – or prevent you from achieving if they hold you back.

This, of course, raises the question, "How does your subconscious mind make you think, feel and act like that?"

How Your Subconscious Shapes Your Thoughts, Feelings and Actions

As mentioned earlier, your subconscious loves identifying patterns, storing them away for future use and then recognising and following those patterns when similar situations arise.

There are three main ways that these patterns are installed in your subconscious: You experience it (either personally or by observing someone else); it is "suggested" to you, usually by an authority figure either when you were a child, or as an adult in a state of heightened emotion; and by repetition (this can install it as a pattern of behaviour or habit, even overriding the unconscious minds' desire to keep you safe).

Experience

The first main way a pattern of behaviour becomes ingrained in your mind is through experience, which can happen in two ways – either by experiencing it firsthand or by witnessing it in someone else.

Experiencing something firsthand is the more obvious of the two. For example, if you're attacked by a dog as a child, your unconscious mind registers the fear and pain, notes that dogs are dangerous and creates a pattern: Whenever you see a dog, you feel afraid and instinctively react with fight, flight or freeze – fulfilling your subconscious' primary role of keeping you safe.

Experiencing something vicariously – through someone else – is when you observe or are made aware of something bad or frightening happening to someone else. For example, if, as a child, you saw a parent scream or flee at the sight of a spider, your subconscious might interpret spiders as dangerous, and, again, you instinctively react with fight, flight or freeze when you see one.

These fears can easily develop into phobias.

Suggestion

Another way that subconscious "programmes" can be set is through suggestion, usually by an authority figure and at a time of heightened emotion or feelings of uncertainty. This is especially true in childhood, when you were under eleven years old and had not developed the critical faculty to assess whether what an authority figure told you was right or wrong.

If a parent, teacher or authority figure once told you that you were useless or would never amount to anything – perhaps after you made a mistake or failed to meet their expectations – your unconscious mind may accept it as fact. This can plant the seeds for anxiety, impostor syndrome and feelings of inadequacy that surface later in life.

Repetition

The third way a pattern can be installed in your subconscious mind is through repetition.

There are so many examples of this in our everyday life, driving being a very obvious one. When you first learned to drive, you had to consciously focus on every step – checking the mirror, signaling, pressing the clutch, shifting gears, applying the accelerator and so on. But through repetition, these actions became automatic. Over time, you needed less and less conscious effort until, eventually, you could drive on "autopilot," barely thinking about your actions. These patterns were installed in your unconscious mind through practice and repetition.

Another example, a negative one this time, is smoking. I have worked with many smokers in my hypnotherapy practice, and I have yet to meet one who enjoyed their first cigarette.

In most cases, that first cigarette made their eyes water, their throat sting, and their body react with coughing and nausea. While some of this may be dismissed as a physical reaction to the smoke, I believe it was also the subconscious mind saying,

"This is dangerous, and I'm making your body react this way to stop you from repeating it and putting yourself in harm's way."

However, those who went on to develop a smoking habit persisted – often due to reasons like wanting to "fit in," peer pressure or wanting to look "cool." Over time, their subconscious mind adapted, thinking, "Well, they keep doing it, so it must be safe," and just like that, the smoking habit took hold.

Every time you experience something, witness an event, hear an authority figure's words or repeatedly engage in a behaviour, your subconscious mind assesses its safety, determines an appropriate response, and stores it in its internal filing cabinet for future reference.

In the future when it sees something or something happens, or it notices that you are in a certain situation, it asks "What's this a bit like?" then instantly, before you even have the chance to think about it consciously, scrolls through its files to find something similar and, based on that, sees how to react to keep you safe (in its view) – starting with fight, flight or freeze. If it believes what you did before kept you safe, it repeats it, resulting in a habitual "thought, feeling, behaviour" pattern programmed into your subconscious.

At this point, it is worth noting that we are only born with two fears – loud noises and falling – so everything else is learned, either from experience or exposure.

Most of the time, your subconscious mind recognising patterns and reacting in its usual way is beneficial. If it weren't, you wouldn't know to run from danger, you'd have to relearn how to drive every time you got in a car, you'd have to figure out how to open a door each time you encountered one slightly different from the last – and you might even have to learn to walk again every time you wanted to go somewhere!

But sometimes, this isn't so helpful. If your subconscious perceives an experience – whether firsthand or learned – as negative, it may file it under "things to fear" or "things to avoid." This can trigger fight, flight or freeze, along with a cascade of thoughts and emotions, causing you to feel and act in ways you neither want nor like.

Using the earlier example of your subconscious learning that spiders are dangerous from a parent's reaction, imagine spotting a piece of black thread on the floor. Your unconscious mind instantly asks, "What's this a bit like?" It scans its internal filing cabinet, finds "spider," retrieves "how to react to a spider," and instructs you to scream and run away – all in a fraction of a second.

Similarly, if a parent or teacher once told you that you were useless, this belief may resurface in adulthood – especially in a business setting. When you feel you might be in trouble, struggle to answer a question from your boss or suspect you've made a mistake, your unconscious mind asks, "What's this a bit like?" It scans its internal filing cabinet and pulls out memories such as "the time I dropped the eggs and Dad said I was an idiot," "the time I wasn't sure what I was doing and the headmaster told me I was useless" or "the time I messed up the maths test and the teacher said I'd never succeed at anything." It then retrieves the associated pattern – "how to react when I've done something wrong" – and, in an instant, triggers that response, making you feel, for example, that you're stupid or not good enough.

As a personal example, I went to a fairly strict school at a time when pupils weren't safeguarded as they are today. Our primary school teacher – who was later alleged to be an alcoholic – subscribed to the belief that "a firm hand" was necessary for discipline. He frequently punished students by making them stretch out their hands and striking them hard with a leather belt for minor infractions, such as forgetting a school book or making a mistake in their work.

One day, he was on a rant about how unobservant we all were. He turned to me and barked, "What's the name of the street outside the school?" When I froze, unable to remember, he lost his temper, grabbed me by the hair, dragged me to the front of the class, and then ordered me outside. I had to walk across the playground – under the watchful eyes of the entire school – read the street sign, and return to announce it to the class.

For years, even decades afterward, I carried an overwhelming fear of making mistakes or not knowing the answer to a question – especially in front of someone senior. I dreaded the possibility of pain or humiliation, which led me to keep my head down, stay quiet and remain as unnoticed as possible in work meetings where I could, and should, have contributed.

Lockdown during the COVID pandemic is another very good example of the power of suggestion by an authority figure. As you have probably noticed, a lot more people, particularly younger ones, are suffering badly from anxiety since lockdown – many don't like being around other people, and others tend to be much more aggressive. Some don't like coming to the office or going to busy places. In my hypnotherapy practice, I have seen many people who feel this way come to me for help overcoming it, so much so that I began to ask myself, "Why do so many people feel like that?"

My conclusion was that, if you think back, here in the UK, we had the Prime Minister and the Health Secretary – two of the most authoritative figures in our adult lives – telling us, at a time of intense emotion, particularly fear, that we had to stay indoors and avoid others. Not only was being near people dangerous and potentially fatal to us, but we were also told that we could be a danger to them, possibly harming or even killing them. That message is now embedded in nearly everyone's subconscious – so it's no wonder people feel anxious!

With patterns that arise as a result of learned experiences or as a result of an authority figure planting the suggestion, it is quite often the case that the person who is "suffering" from the consequences cannot recall the original event at all. They are at a loss to understand or explain why they think, feel and act the way they do.

In his great book *Healing: Beyond Pills and Potions,* Dr. Steve Bierman looks at how the power of the authority figure can be harnessed positively.[1] He uses it in a clinical setting to achieve outcomes that would seem impossible in mainstream medicine. He believes that the subconscious of a person in a state of heightened emotion – in his case, a patient in the emergency room who is deathly afraid – is actively looking for an authority figure to guide them and tell them what to do. As a doctor, he deliberately assumes that authority and provides the patient with suggestions around healing and wellness. This has demonstrated fantastic results, including pain and blood-free surgery, stopping bleeding, healing fractures and even correcting heart arrhythmia.

Now that we know how these subconscious patterns are formed, how do we go about changing them?

Changing Limiting Beliefs and Patterns

As you have probably gathered by now, all change happens at a subconscious level. In hypnotherapy, there's a saying: Conscious awareness does not lead to therapeutic change.

Think again of that person with a fear of flying. They know, logically, that air travel is statistically safer than something as routine as walking to the shops – but that knowledge does nothing to stop their fear. It's the same with anxiety, impostor syndrome or a fear of public speaking. You understand there's no real danger, that your feelings don't reflect reality, and that others handle these situations just fine – yet that awareness alone doesn't help you overcome them.

So it's not reality that is the problem; it is your subconscious thoughts about reality.

To address these issues effectively, we must go beyond the limitations of the conscious mind and reach the subconscious – the part that's creating the "problem" in the first place. By working at that level, we can rewire neural pathways, making all change possible.

As I mentioned earlier, your thoughts and feelings shape your actions and behaviors, which in turn determine your outcomes. Change your thoughts, and you'll change your emotions, shift your behaviors and start achieving better results.

We will look at ways of doing this as we go through the ASDIC Framework.

How We Think

Before I get to that, I would like to spend a bit of time looking at how we think and how we store and process information. That, too, is important to understand as we embark on the change journey.

So how do we do that?

Well, we think and process information in five Representation Systems – or Rep Systems – which coincide with our senses. Visual (pictures and movies), Auditory (sounds), Kinaesthetic (feelings), Olfactory (smell) and Gustatory (taste). However, we work primarily in three of these: Visual, Auditory and Kinaesthetic, often referred to as VAK.

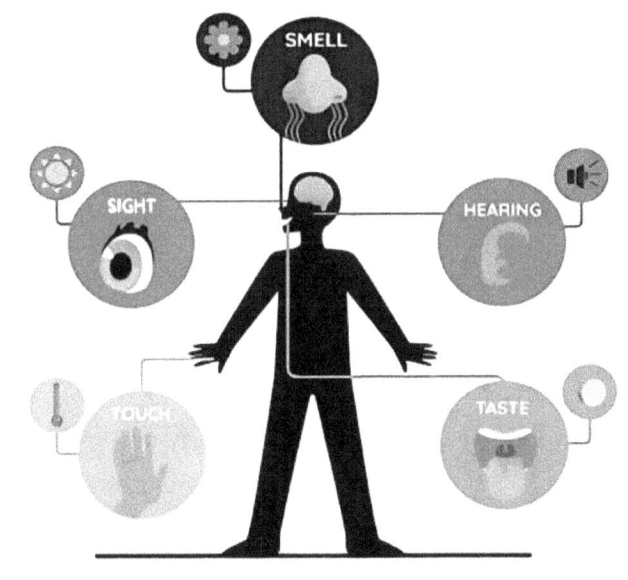

I'll talk a lot more about the benefits of understanding and learning how to use other people's Rep systems later.

Even within VAK, pictures and words or sounds are generally key to creating feelings and emotions.

Looking at the systems in reverse order, words are, simply put, the internal chatter and self-talk that go on in our heads – the stories that we tell and scenarios we create for ourselves. As anyone who has experienced negative self-talk will testify, this chatter in our heads can easily intensify and run out of control, getting louder and faster, going round and round in a vicious circle, creating a negative vortex and leaving you feeling that all you want is for it to stop.

In this state, it is easier to think things like "I am a stupid person" rather than "I am a good person who maybe did a stupid thing" or "I am a bad person" rather than "I am a good person who did a bad thing" – ultimately believing that because of that, disaster will surely follow.

It hardwires that program into your brain.

Beyond words, we display pictures and play movies inside our heads – and these can dramatically affect our mental state as well. I talked earlier about the effect of the lockdown on the psyche of many people. When you think about it, over the last few years, we have had plenty of opportunities to play out scary movies and catastrophic movies in our heads. These movies often focus on a worst-case scenario and blow it out of all proportion, frightening us and putting us into a state of anxiety at a subconscious level, even though these events are likely to never happen. To compound things, your subconscious can't tell the difference between experiences that are real and those that are vividly imagined, so you can easily be affected by things that have existed only inside your head.

How do we escape from the state we get ourselves into when we combine these pictures, words and feelings? In most cases, very easily, as it happens!

When we understand these rep systems and how they work, we can use NLP techniques – particularly one known as Submodalities, which I look at in Chapter 5 – to train our minds and bodies to remove any negative states and replace them with more beneficial and helpful ones.

Chapter Recap

We have a conscious mind and a subconscious mind, and they do different things. The subconscious mind controls most of what you think, feel and do, and the results that you get, every day. All lasting change occurs at a subconscious level. Most of the time, communication between the two parts is one-directional, where the subconscious mind can very much affect the conscious mind, but it doesn't work the other way around. Thus, in order to work with the subconscious, you have to bypass the conscious mind.

We think and process information in five Rep systems – Visual, Auditory, Kinaesthetic, Olfactory and Gustatory. Visual, Auditory and Kinaesthetic are the Rep systems that we use most, as we use words and pictures to create feelings. By changing the way that we construct the words, pictures and feelings, we can change the way we feel – which changes the way we act and the outcomes that we get.

Chapter 3
The ASDIC Framework

"We cannot solve our problems with the same thinking we used when we created them."
– Albert Einstein

In this chapter, I introduce the ASDIC Framework – a unique therapeutic and developmental approach that I developed by blending the knowledge, skills and insights I gathered from my corporate experience with my work as a therapist.

Now that we understand how our mind works, it's easier to see how past experiences and suggestions – whether from ourselves or others – shape our beliefs and contribute to the negative patterns we adopt, which can manifest in various ways. Among aspiring executives – and business people in general – the most common of these include impostor syndrome, fear of failure, self-doubt about skills and abilities, a sense of not "belonging," anxiety (either general or specific) and a fear of public speaking.

This is far from an exhaustive list, and I have also come across other limiting beliefs and patterns, such as fear of looking stupid, fear of success (it is a thing!) and feeling stuck.

These present themselves in many ways. In Appendix 1, I have set out a matrix of the most common beliefs and patterns, the different ways they can present (the "symptoms" if you like) and matched the symptoms to the beliefs and patterns. While putting a name to the underlying beliefs and patterns can be an interesting exercise, it has little to no relevance to the techniques we use to overcome them.

People who exhibit all or some of these symptoms and behaviours can be perceived (wrongly) by others as disengaged or uncooperative, defensive or even lacking ambition or drive.

It was when clients had been coming to me for a while, seeking help to overcome these negative beliefs and patterns, or, in some cases, the symptoms, that I realised there was a massive crossover between my experience in the corporate world and my experience in the world of hypnotherapy and NLP.

These people wanted to change not just their negative beliefs and patterns but also the success and life they enjoy. Change was a common theme across both the corporate and the therapy worlds.

There are many models of change – just Google "Models of Change" and be amazed. I have worked with and been involved in many of them, but my favourite – explained to me by my friend and mentor Paul Russell – does not appear in any textbooks, so far as I am aware. Paul was a plain-speaking Welshman, and the model, called the 4FU model, reflects that.

The 4 FU Model

This model represents the four stages of emotion during the change journey from feeling stuck, through to thriving

- Fear & Uncertainty (FU1)
- Blaming External Forces (FU2)
- Forwards & Upwards (FU4)
- Blaming your internal limiting beliefs (FU3)

The first FU is Fear & Uncertainty. Something is not right, and you know change has to happen. But you don't know what it means for you.

The second FU is "F**K You, external forces." It can't be your fault that something's not right, so you blame everyone and everything else. Maybe you convince yourself that your boss has got it in for you or your colleagues have been undermining you. The bottom line is you believe it's certainly not your fault!

The Third FU is "F**K You, my internal limiting beliefs and patterns." The light has come on and you've realised maybe there is something in you holding you back and stopping you from achieving what you want. At first, you think it is something in you and, therefore, you can't do anything about it. "It's just the way I am," you think, and the anger at that either drags you down for the rest of your career – or drives you to look for ways to overcome it and move on to...

The Fourth FU, "Forwards and Upwards." Once you have overcome the limiting beliefs and patterns, the sky's the limit, and you feel yourself accelerating onwards and upwards in your career.

Frankly, most frustrated but ambitious executives and business people are in the FU3 quadrant, looking for ways to overcome the limiting beliefs and patterns they know are holding them back. Certainly, that is where most of the people who come to me looking for help find themselves.

As the people I worked with started to get results, seeing their careers developing and becoming more successful, I realised almost all of them were responding to very similar approaches within a structured framework that I had developed – a combination of hypnotherapy, NLP and practical work. I took this framework, analysed it and codified it into what is now the

ASDIC Framework. I have since used the ASDIC Framework with both individual and corporate clients in therapy sessions, coaching sessions and training days.

The ASDIC Framework looks like this:

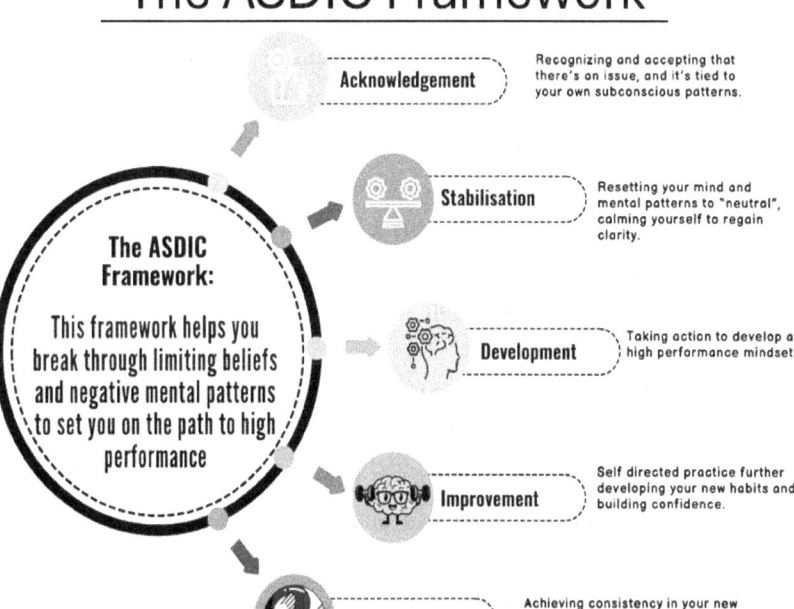

In this and the following chapters, we will look at the stages of this framework, the processes and interventions that can be used and the skills that can be learned at each stage – some of which you will be able to do on your own, others which require some external involvement (and I will provide links to audio files for these).

Why ASDIC? The answer goes back to my childhood and the stories my father used to tell me about World War II submarines. I'm not sure why he told so many submarine stories – he was too young (just) to be involved in the war, and my grandfather served in the Merchant Navy. Perhaps it was because, as a merchant seaman on the convoys between the UK and Russia, there was a constant fear of attack by German submarines. If you've ever watched a WWII submarine film, you'll recognise those tense moments when the crew, aware that an enemy is nearby, falls into absolute silence – only to hear the distinctive "ping." That "ping" is ASDIC in action!

Also known as sonar, it was a pivotal – and at the time, pioneering – technology that enabled vessels to detect and locate ships, underwater obstacles and enemy submarines. ASDIC worked by emitting sound waves and analysing their echoes as they bounced back, allowing vessels to pinpoint the position, distance and movement of underwater threats or targets.

This detection system provided critical situational awareness, enabling vessels to either evade the enemy or strategically position themselves to launch or defend against an attack. In a chaotic and hostile environment, ASDIC gave submarines a clear advantage in determining their position relative to both friendly and hostile vessels, allowing them to act decisively and effectively.

I saw this as a powerful metaphor for how individuals can navigate their own lives and careers. Just as ASDIC technology provides feedback from the environment to help a vessel determine its location and trajectory – and take appropriate, effective action – the ASDIC Framework enables individuals to use self-reflection, feedback from experiences and input from others to assess where they stand in their personal and professional lives. It helps them gain a clear understanding of their strengths, weaknesses and the opportunities or threats they face. This heightened self-awareness can mean the difference between drifting aimlessly and making informed, strategic choices to create the career, success and life they desire.

Moreover, ASDIC is not just about detection; it's about decision-making. A vessel equipped with ASDIC can choose whether to avoid a threat, engage with it or take a different course altogether – whichever will be of the greatest benefit. Similarly, when individuals become more aware of their internal and external environments, they can make better decisions regarding their goals and challenges. They can identify limiting beliefs, unproductive patterns or external factors that might impede their progress and take appropriate action to overcome or avoid these barriers.

In essence, it empowers them to move forward with purpose – much like a vessel navigating uncertain waters – helping them avoid or overcome dangers safely and confidently, ready for the next challenge.

In both contexts, it is awareness and taking action based on that awareness that leads to better outcomes. When individuals know where they stand, understand the obstacles and opportunities within and around them, and know they are equipped to deal with them, they are better positioned to steer their lives and careers in the direction they choose.

Let's look at each phase of the framework.

Acceptance

As I mentioned above, the 4FU Model really kicks in at Stage 3 – when you realise, acknowledge and accept that the issue is with you and is not someone else's doing. Note that I say "the issue is with you," not "you are the issue" – more on that later.

It can be difficult to reach that realisation and acceptance, and some people never do.

One of the most common indicators that the issue may be with you is when you realise that the pattern – the thoughts, feelings, behaviours or results – keeps repeating in similar situations, even though the environment and people around you have changed.

As mentioned earlier, this is not your fault. You are simply acting out a pattern ingrained in you from a young age. Remember that tale of my alcoholic teacher? It had been ingrained in my subconscious by that experience (and probably others that I can't consciously remember) that getting something wrong or not knowing the correct answer was dangerous as it led to pain and humiliation, so my subconscious did its very best to keep me safe by making sure that I did not put myself in that position.

Stabilisation

Once you have acknowledged and accepted that the issue is yours and have resolved to do something about it, the first step is to stabilise yourself and get back to neutral – the "zero" on that scale of minus ten to plus ten that I talked about in the introduction. You can probably also think about it as being like a "factory reset." You didn't come into this world with these fears, beliefs, habits and patterns, you just developed them through the years. Now, it's time to get rid of them!

This is the hardest and most important phase. Once you have stabilised and are no longer being dragged down or held back by your limiting beliefs, negative habits and patterns, it feels like a great weight has been lifted off your shoulders (sorry – I love a mixed metaphor) and the sense of freedom that it gives sets you up for more.

The Stabilisation phase involves a lot of mindset work, removing those negative patterns and limiting beliefs installed so long ago. This is primarily done through hypnotherapy and NLP techniques, but affirmations can also help.

A further element of the Stabilisation phase and subsequent phases is learning techniques for dealing with anxiety so you can find out which works best for you. While hypnotherapy and NLP techniques can help with anxiety, they will not remove it completely – nor should they. Anxiety can be a defence mechanism, and there are times when it is ok to be anxious. However, when anxiety does rear its head, it is great to have some techniques in your back pocket that will put that beast back in its box!

Chapters 4 to 8 cover many of the techniques that I use to help deal with anxiety. These techniques are not phase-specific but are designed to give you a range of techniques to try.

Development

Once you are "reset" and have moved the arrow from a minus number to zero, it is time to start moving forward – pushing the arrow from zero to ten.

This is generally easier than pushing the arrow from a negative number to zero, both because you have overcome blocks, limiting beliefs and negative patterns holding you back and because your mind has become accustomed to the practices needed.

In this phase of the ASDIC Framework, you continue some of the techniques from the Stabilisation phase, as well as introduce new techniques and start to develop more practical knowledge and skills, such as motivation and goal setting.

Improvement

The Improvement phase of the ASDIC Framework goes hand in hand with the Development phase.

In the Development phase, you will begin using new techniques and learning new, practical knowledge and skills. You will also start to see results.

However, these tools and techniques are not "one-off." You will need to work at them continuously to become better at them and to start integrating them seamlessly into your life. Improvement is the stage of repetition, to change practices and mindsets from something that you consciously do to something that happens automatically. In other words, you embed it as a habit, a belief or a pattern in your unconscious mind.

As you will remember from Chapter 2, "repetition" is one of the three main ways that things can be installed in your unconscious mind. You will effectively be using the same techniques the mind uses when a person starts driving. At first, they have a myriad things they have to think about and consciously remember to do every time they get behind the wheel of a car, whereas after driving repeatedly over a number of months and years, it becomes something that they can do every day without thinking about or even noticing they are doing it.

We will also look at developing good working relationships in this phase, particularly focusing on rapport, trust and communication.

Consistency

The outcome of your work in the Stabilisation, Development and Improvement phases will be that you are set up to consistently and congruently use the tools and skills that you have learned so that your thoughts, feelings, actions and behaviours align – all working together to give you the results that you want and deserve.

However, staying consistent can be a battle, as life and people can easily throw you off balance. When that happens, it's easy to revert to old patterns your subconscious once saw as "safe." That's why we'll explore ways to handle difficult people and situations differently – approaching them with a more positive mindset – in this phase.

If you feel yourself slipping from your new way of thinking, feeling or behaving, simply identify the issue and revisit the relevant part of this book. Use the resources, audio files, or exercises to reinforce your progress, and you'll soon be back on track, congruently firing on all cylinders!

So that is the ASDIC Framework. Now for the interesting part: implementing it. In the following chapters, we look at the tools and techniques, each broken down by which phase or phases of the framework they are best used. Some will apply to more than one phase.

As you will see, some of these are all about changing your mindset, removing and changing the limiting beliefs, habits and patterns holding you back and adopting new, positive ones that enable you to drive towards the success you know you are capable of and deserve. Others are practical advice, guidance and exercises to help you gain and develop the knowledge and skills that successful people enjoy.

Chapter Recap

As you look for ways to overcome limiting beliefs, thoughts, habits and patterns that are holding you back, you are on a change journey. If you have read this far, you are probably in Quadrant 3 of the 4FU model and have realised that it is something in you that has been holding you back, not other people or some external factor.

The ASDIC framework was developed to help people just like you, guiding you through these five key phases:

- **Acceptance.** Recognising and accepting that there is an issue and it is tied to your subconscious patterns.

- **Stabilisation.** Getting your mind back to a clear or reset position. Reset your mind and mental patterns to "neutral," calming yourself to gain clarity.

- **Development.** Starting to create new pathways, mindsets, patterns and behaviours.

- **Improvement.** Expanding your skills and improving your interactions and relationships with others.

- **Consistency.** Becoming consistent in your new approach, developing resilience to difficult people and situations.

Chapter 4
Acceptance

> *"You can't change what you refuse to confront."*
> – Unknown

As I mentioned in the previous chapter, acceptance is the first step in the ASDIC model – and also one of the hardest. It requires recognising and accepting uncomfortable truths about the beliefs you hold and the patterns you follow, even if many of these operate at a subconscious level.

Acceptance means acknowledging and then accepting that *you* have a problem; that it is the beliefs, thoughts, feelings and behaviours inside you causing you to struggle to get the success you want and deserve – even though these likely come from your subconscious.

This can be particularly challenging because once these truths (and the issues they are causing) are recognised, many people hesitate to discuss them openly for fear of being seen as weak or somehow "damaged." In my corporate training sessions, for instance, I have stopped asking participants what they feel is holding them back or if they have any limiting beliefs or patterns of behaviour, as they do not want to admit such things in front of colleagues or supervisors. Interestingly, once the sessions are over and participants have seen first-hand the impact the techniques can have, they are generally only too keen to discuss their issues. It is not uncommon for many to sign up for private sessions.

One of the most common indicators that the issue may be deeply ingrained within you is when you realise that the pattern – the thoughts, feelings, behaviours or the results – keeps recurring in similar situations, even though the environment and the people around you have changed.

As a personal example, I realised that the issue came from within me at a meeting in Boston. I was well aware that I rarely spoke up in management meetings. I had convinced myself that no one wanted to hear from "the lawyer" (as I was at the time) or that others talked or loved the sound of their own voices so much that there was never a natural pause for me to contribute. I reassured myself that I would speak up if I had something truly meaningful to say.

Being at least somewhat self-aware, I recognised that my quietness could be seen as a lack of drive, confidence or ability – all potential career limiters. So, when I was promoted to global legal lead for one of the company's core operating groups, I resolved to change that and become a proactive contributor in management meetings. I started off well, but before long, I slipped back into old habits, retreating into my shell and sitting quietly in the corner.

It was at that point I realised that this was not someone else's fault or someone else's problem. It dawned on me that this pattern had repeated itself so often in different situations that the only logical conclusion was that the cause wasn't the environment or other people – it was something within me.

And, as it is for anyone, it was a tough realisation. Your first thought is usually, "Why am I like this? I'm just as smart as (almost) everyone else, and I have plenty to offer."

It's easy to accept it as "just the way I am" and resign yourself to a career of frustration, never fully realising your potential. In other words, reaching the level of acknowledgement is easy – but what matters is what you choose to accept. Do you (wrongly) accept that there's nothing you can do about it, as so many do? Or do you accept its presence while committing to overcoming and changing it?

The key to which route you take is to realise that the issue is "with you" and not "you." The thoughts, feelings, behaviours and patterns are something that you do, not something that you are. The patterns and behaviours are the result of a process that your mind goes through, not a thing or a part of your identity. This is a key point.

As discussed, the root of these recurring patterns often lies in past experiences or suggestions made by authority figures, whether remembered consciously or not, or, indeed, whether it actually happened – it may well be a false (but vivid) memory. Remarkably, imagined events can sometimes affect the subconscious in the same way as real ones, making acknowledgement and acceptance even more complex.

Once an issue is recognised, it can be tempting to spend a lot of time and effort delving into the past, searching for its cause (often referred to as the "Initial Sensitising Event" or "ISE"). However, this is often frustrating and, from a practical standpoint, usually unnecessary – and sometimes counterproductive – to linger on examining the past. While identifying the origin of negative behaviours or beliefs can sometimes be beneficial, the primary focus should be on the future: defining and building the thoughts, feelings and behaviours that will set the patterns to drive your future success.

In rare cases, it may be necessary to revisit past events to find the ISE. This must be approached with great care, as reconnecting with a traumatic memory risks re-traumatizing the sufferer, potentially worsening the thoughts and feelings. For this reason, hypnotherapy and NLP (unlike other approaches) generally avoid techniques that could provoke such reactions, and I am not including any of them in this book. When past experiences do need to be revisited, these must be done only under the supervision of a qualified, professional therapist to ensure that the client remains in a safe, dissociated state, viewing the events from a detached perspective that reduces emotional impact.

In most instances, however, it is neither necessary nor particularly helpful to relive past events in order to resolve current challenges. While understanding the origin of a limiting belief can sometimes offer clarity, the focus should remain on creating the desired outcomes moving forward.

In any case, the essential first step in overcoming limiting thoughts, feelings and behaviour patterns is to acknowledge that an issue exists and that it lies within your power to address it. Once you have done this, you are ready to move forward into the Development stage.

In the same vein, it is not always necessary (although it may be helpful and comforting) to put a "label" on the issue. While conditions like impostor syndrome and doubt about your skills and abilities have different features (see Appendix 1), in many cases, the approach to dealing with them is the same. For that reason, I have, for the most part, included in this book techniques by phase of the ASDIC Framework, where the underlying themes are often the same, rather than by specific condition.

Tools and Techniques for This Phase

While there are no tools and techniques specific to this phase of the ASDIC framework – other than noticing how and when you think, feel or act in unhelpful ways – recognising which of them repeat themselves in different situations and acknowledging this may be a problem that is with you will help greatly. Anxiety can be a constant companion throughout the process.

Dealing With Anxiety

Although anxiety has many definitions, it's a bit like a yeti – you know it when you see it (or, more likely, feel it). It's that awful sense of unease and worry, a dread of the future or an upcoming event, often accompanied by intrusive negative thoughts and nervous behaviours or symptoms like pacing, tightness in the stomach or chest, restlessness, fatigue, shortness of breath or difficulty concentrating.

While it can be crippling at times, anxiety can serve a positive purpose in certain situations, so we do not want to eliminate it completely. We need to have tools and techniques we can use to manage it when it does arise, whether warranted or not.

In the chapters for each of the phases of the framework, I will introduce a different technique for dealing with anxiety very quickly. Different techniques work better for different people, so it's worth trying them all to find the one that reduces your anxiety most quickly and effectively.

They are generally techniques you can use "in the moment," when you feel the anxiety coming on and, for many people, provide a quick fix allowing them to remain, or return to, calm.

The first technique is known as bilateral stimulation. This is a technique that you can use almost anytime and anywhere you feel anxious. I will go through the technique and then talk about how it works.

To start, pick up something that you can easily hold in your hand. A ball around the size of a tennis ball is particularly good, but really, you can use whatever is at hand – a pen, a phone, a small water bottle, anything.

Rate your anxiety on a scale of 1 to 10, where 10 is the worst anxiety possible and 1 is no anxiety at all.

Hold your arms in front of your body, with the object in one hand.

Swing your arm and hand holding the object out to the side, then bring it back in. Just after your hand crosses the midline of your body, pass the object to your other hand and swing that arm out to the opposite side, keeping the hand that just passed the object in front of you.

Continue this motion, passing the object from one hand to the other just after it crosses the midline, then swinging the arm and hand holding the object out to the side before bringing it back in.

Do this for a minute, stop, take a deep breath and rate your anxiety on a scale of 1 to 10 again. You may well notice that the anxiety has reduced.

Keep repeating this process until the anxiety has gone, or at least reached a level at which you are comfortable.

How does it work?

As you may know, the right side of your brain controls the left side of your body, and the left side of your brain controls the right side of your body.

Anxiety generally sits in your unconscious mind, which, very broadly, you can imagine as equating to the right side of your brain. When anxiety strikes, that part of the brain becomes very active, as all of the focus goes on to the anxiety and the fight, flight, freeze response.

In simple terms, bilateral stimulation uses the mind-body connection to also activate the left side of the brain at the same time, meaning that the focus on the anxiety – and the associated electrical activity in that part of your brain – is dissipated across both parts of the brain.

In the mind-body connection, what happens in your mind can trigger physical reactions in your body. For example, if you're watching a scary film where the hero searches for the villain in a dark, silent house – tense music playing, a floorboard creaking – you might find your heart racing, your body tensed and even feel a hint of sweat, despite knowing it's just a film. You may also notice this effect in the next chapter when you try the "taste the lemon" exercise.

However, just as your mind can influence your body, the reverse is also true – physical actions can affect your mental state, with power posing being a prime example.

This is why bilateral stimulation is so effective. The object's movement across both sides of your body stimulates activity across both sides of your brain, relieving the overload on the right, anxiety-causing side.

Chapter Recap

Acknowledging that there is an issue – and it is something in you – can be difficult and uncomfortable, but knowing the specific source of an issue is not always necessary. Once you have acknowledged it, you need to accept that it is there – and that you need to deal with it if you want to move on. The focus is on defining a future state and achieving the outcomes you desire rather than dwelling on the past.

Chapter 5
Stabilisation

"When we are no longer able to change a situation, we are challenged to change ourselves."
– Viktor Frankl

Once you have acknowledged and accepted that there is an issue (at least one!) and that it is causing unnecessary negative beliefs, thoughts, feelings, behaviours and patterns to occur repeatedly for you, the next step is to stabilise, remove these issues and reset to neutral. That is, reset to 0 from a negative number on my "-10 to +10" scale.

We generally don't enjoy or appreciate these negative beliefs and thoughts and want them to calm down or stop. But the more we try to quiet them, the more they seem to take over – often flying around endlessly in our heads. "I just want the noise in my head to stop" is a common phrase! However, rarely does agitating something calm it down. I tend to think of it like a snow globe. When you shake one, the blizzard of "snowflakes" gets worse; leave it still, and the blizzard eventually settles and calm returns.

The Stabilisation phase is about adopting the Snow Globe Model – calming your racing thoughts and restoring a sense of stability. It's about simply feeling normal again – not like an impostor or unworthy, not feeling that you don't belong, or that you are anxious, negative or overwhelmed. It's about easing the burdens that weigh you down and keep you from achieving the outcomes you want and deserve.

As you'll have gathered from earlier chapters, most – if not all – of these underlying issues have been with you for a long time, deeply embedded in your subconscious by past experiences or "suggestions" from authority figures during moments of heightened emotion. Because of this, overcoming them through willpower alone is difficult, if not impossible. To address them effectively – and ideally, quickly, depending on their depth and complexity – therapeutic techniques are needed. In this chapter, I'll explore examples, focusing on NLP, hypnotherapy and psycho-sensory techniques known as Havening Techniques®.

If you are a bit wary of these techniques and want to try to rid yourself of the issues without them, I would suggest that repetition, combined with self-suggestion and affirmation – and a good chunk of "fake it 'til you make it" – is probably the way that has the greatest chance of success.

What does that look like in practice? Well, the best example that I can give is about a friend of mine – I'll call him Jeff –

who was an associate partner at one of the firms I worked at. Associate partner was a sort of halfway role between being a senior manager and a full-blown equity partner. An equity partner was an owner of the business, a boss who took home good money. Associate Partners almost all wanted to be partners, but most fell by the wayside. One day, we noticed that Jeff had started dressing a bit differently – sharper and smarter. He was speaking to people more directly and seemed to be distancing himself from colleagues. When this was pointed out to him, he responded, "I want to be a partner, and if you want to be a partner, you have to act like a partner."

While we were taken aback at the time – this was not the Jeff that we had come to know – his thinking was spot on. He did become a partner and moved on to become a very senior and well-respected one.

If you want to attempt to overcome the issues that are holding you back from achieving the success that you seek purely by willpower, I believe there are two things that you need to do.

Start dressing and behaving like you already have that success. This will feel very uncomfortable for some time as your unconscious mind tries to keep you "safe," and you may alienate some of the people who knew the "old" you but never waver from it. Be like that every day until, with repetition, your unconscious mind accepts that that is now the way you are and that it is "safe" to be that way. This approach also ties into the mind-body connection mentioned in the previous chapter. As you start acting as if you already have that success through your demeanour, posture and speech, your mind responds to those cues, creating a cycle of positive reinforcement.

Give yourself daily affirmations that you have achieved success or are making progress toward it. Perhaps the best-known affirmation is "Every day, in every way, I am getting better and better," first quoted by French psychologist Émile Coué in the late 1800s, likely in his book *Self Mastery Through Conscious Autosuggestion*. He was a pioneer in the field of autosuggestion, believing that by repeating positive affirmations, you can train your subconscious to quiet negative inner thoughts that may hold you back from achieving your goals. This same principle applies to setting and achieving goals, which we'll explore in more detail later.

(Also, contrary to what a participant in one of my courses suggested, Coué's affirmation did not originate with Frank Spencer in the UK sitcom *Some Mothers Do 'Ave 'Em!*).

Should you want to take the plunge and find out more about therapeutic techniques, read on! I will focus on NLP and hypnotherapy, and also introduce you to the concept of Havening and add another technique for dealing with anxiety to your toolbox.

NLP

What is NLP? Many, many books have been written on the subject, so what follows is my distilled version:

NLP (Neuro Linguistic Programming) is like an operating manual for your mind, blending psychology and linguistics to help reshape thought patterns, emotional responses and behaviours. Richard Bandler and John Grinder first developed it while studying the mental "programs" that allowed top athletes to achieve performance levels others – identical in every other way – could only dream of.[2] As their research progressed, they discovered that these "programs" could not only be created and modified but also had much broader therapeutic applications.

Using NLP techniques, you can reprogram your mind to change mental states. For example, you can use it to overcome the overpowering state of fear that comes with a phobia or to overcome a state of stress and doubt and even pivot it to a state of confidence and clarity. Unlike many complex therapies that require numerous, lengthy sessions, NLP offers simple strategies that can often create a noticeable shift within minutes.

Here is a fairly simple NLP process – based on the concepts of submodalities and anchoring – that you can use to "switch off" a negative state:

To begin, set the negative state that you want to change. If you are not already in the negative state that you want to change, recall it – make sure you have got it back before you start. If that state happens rarely, recall the first, worst and most recent time you had it.

Next, breathe deeply and close your eyes. Notice what you see, hear and feel in that state. Calibrate the feeling on a scale of

1 to 10, where 10 is "It's the worst imaginable" and 1 is "It's barely noticeable."

Focus on the visual images. If they're in colour, turn them black and white. If they're moving, make them still. If you're seeing them through your own eyes, step outside yourself and view them as an observer. Gradually shrink them smaller and smaller until they're tiny, then imagine launching them far into the distance.

Next, shift your attention to the sounds, whether external or internal self-talk. If they're fast, slow them to a normal pace. If they're loud, picture turning a volume dial down to zero.

Now, focus on the feelings. Imagine they have a shape and colour – alter them to the ones you prefer. If they're moving, slow them down or reverse their direction. If they feel rough or spiky, smooth them out. If they're heavy, lighten them. Keep shrinking them until they're tiny, then imagine popping them out of your body, tying them to a helium balloon, and watching them drift away into the sky.

Calibrate the feeling again. Rate it on the same scale of 1 to 10 as before. If it is still 3 or over, repeat the previous step. If it is 2 or less, move to the next step.

Set your anchor – choose a physical action, such as pinching your thumb and forefinger together (unless you've already set that as your "positive" anchor), and hold it for a count of eight. This movement will link the new state to your anchor.

Repeat the process twice more. If progress feels slow, experiment with adjusting different elements, such as adding a border to the visual image.

Finally, test it. When you need a boost, repeat the action to trigger the new state instantly.

The Concepts Behind It

NLP isn't just "positive thinking"; it's a method rooted in how our brain naturally forms patterns. Our minds respond quickly to sensory inputs, and through NLP, you can tap into the subconscious to create new, empowering neural pathways. Anchoring connects physical actions with mental states, and reframing reprograms your cognitive response to external events, allowing you to change your emotional reaction.

Another way to understand this – especially when overcoming negative states – is to think of your brain as having a "recipe" for that state. This recipe is made up of pictures, sounds and feelings known as "modalities," with finer details called "submodalities" (eg whether images are bright or dull, still or moving, or how loud the sounds are). By adjusting these submodalities, you change the recipe, preventing it from producing the negative state – just as swapping out flour in a cake recipe would stop it from making a cake. Once you "anchor" the new recipe, the negative state disappears!

Why does anchoring work? Anchoring leverages your brain's ability to form associations between sensory inputs and emotional states. Over time, this creates a shortcut your brain uses to replicate those emotions with a simple physical cue.

Why does it work so quickly? The true power of NLP lies in how it operates within the framework of the brain's neuroplasticity – the ability to reorganise itself by forming new neural connections. These techniques don't require extensive practice or complex tools; they rely on simple neurological triggers already familiar to our subconscious. This makes NLP perfect for fast state changes, even when you're in the middle of a busy day.

Try it. Next time you feel a need to get into a positive mood or break a negative "state," take a 5-minute break and practice these techniques. Notice the shift in your mood and mental clarity. These quick moments of mental reset can empower you to tackle whatever comes next with greater ease and confidence.

A recent example of the power and speed of submodalities and anchoring – albeit in a slightly different context – came from a hypnotherapy session with a client. After we had finished, she casually mentioned that she was supposed to inject herself weekly for another condition but struggled to do so. The smell of the antiseptic swab she had to use before injecting made her feel so nauseous that she couldn't go through with it.

I told her we would sort it out and then asked her to get one of the swabs. She opened it and smelled it to recreate the problem state and immediately gagging. She rated the feeling at a 9. We then did a submodalities session, incorporating taste and smell, following the approach outlined earlier. It took about 5 to 10 minutes.

When we finished, I asked her to rate the feeling again. She looked at me in amazement and said, "It's gone. It's a zero." We anchored that! "Good," I said. "Now let's test it. Pick up the swab again and smell it." She did and felt none of the nausea that had plagued her before. Later, she told me she had no further issues with her injections.

Hypnosis and Hypnotherapy

Hypnosis is another great tool for creating lasting change quickly – whether to remove limiting beliefs such as impostor syndrome, anxiety or fear of failure in your business life or to help you with personal challenges, like overcoming a phobia or quitting smoking.

In addition to running a hypnotherapy practice, I occasionally perform comedy hypnosis shows. During these shows, I have people believe their feet are stuck to the floor, forget a number or even their own name. While these skits get plenty of laughs, the underlying message is powerful: If hypnosis can stop us from doing things that are core to our being – walking, counting and knowing our name – in just a matter of minutes, imagine how powerful it can be in quickly removing limiting beliefs and negative patterns!

In shows, I always completely remove the suggestions that cause these comic outcomes, returning everyone to their original state. However, after therapy sessions, the suggestions remain, creating the lasting changes my clients come to me for.

What Is Hypnosis?

Ask five different hypnotists, and you will get six different definitions or explanations! The one which resonates most with me is this: "An altered, relaxed, state of consciousness characterised by the bypassing of the critical faculties and increased responsiveness to suggestion."

Under hypnosis, suggestions bypass the critical faculties of normal consciousness, which typically act as a "gatekeeper" between the conscious and subconscious minds. Instead, they enter the subconscious directly. If accepted, the person then acts on them.

Common Questions About Hypnosis

I am asked several questions regularly, mostly based on myths or from having watched a hypnosis comedy show.

Can anyone be hypnotised? Yes, anyone can be hypnotised, as long as they want to be and have the ability to concentrate. A hypnotherapist cannot force you to go into hypnosis against your will.

Can hypnosis make me do things that I don't want to do? Hypnosis cannot make you do anything that you do not want to do or that is contrary to your moral or ethical values.

Will I lose control? In hypnosis, you are still in control at all times; you always know what is happening, and you can come out at any time.

Will I be asleep or unconscious? No. Hypnosis is not sleep. Hypnosis will not make you unconscious. You always know what is happening.

Will hypnosis make me lose my memory? No. Hypnosis will not make you lose your memory.

Can hypnosis make me reveal my deepest, darkest secrets? No. It cannot make you reveal your inner secrets.

Can I get stuck in hypnosis? No. You will always come out of hypnosis. Even if you lose communication with the hypnotist (like if a Zoom link crashes), you will come out of hypnosis on your own in a relatively short period of time.

Pre-Hypnosis Exercises

Before I share the link to a hypnosis session, here are three fun exercises that will examine your powers of focus, imagination and visualisation – all of which contribute to how readily our unconscious mind opens up to suggestions. You may also hear them referred to as "suggestibility tests."

So, if you are curious about how good your powers of focus, imagination and visualisation are or how suggestible you might be, read on – and feel free to try these at home! They don't require any special setup, and each exercise is gentle and engaging. No special training is required, so you can also use them to entertain and impress people at parties! Let's dive in.

And don't worry if nothing happens. They are far from dispositive, and just about everyone can be hypnotised.

Taste the Lemon

This classic test is perfect for discovering how vividly you can imagine sensations and feelings and is a great illustration of the mind-body connection.

What to do: Close your eyes and imagine yourself holding a bright yellow, juicy lemon in your hand. Picture yourself slicing it open, releasing a burst of citrus aroma as the juice runs out. Now, cut it into quarters and bring one to your mouth. Take a big bite – feel the tangy juice flood your tongue, taste its sharpness and notice the sensation as it fills your mouth.

How to judge your reaction: If you feel a twinge in your jaw, a puckering sensation, or even start salivating, it's a sign you have a powerful imagination. If you start salivating, note that your body is reacting to something created solely in your imagination. This is common in many situations and is a clear example of the mind-body connection.

Magnetic Fingers

The Magnetic Fingers exercise explores your ability to focus and how vivid your imagination is, and again checks how readily your body responds to mental cues.

What to do: Hold your arms straight out in front of you, palms facing inward. Clasp your hands together, interlocking your fingers so that the fingers of one hand rest between the knuckles of the other. Squeeze tightly. Now bend your elbows to 90 degrees, positioning your thumbs in front of your eyes.

Raise your index fingers so they are about an inch apart. Focus on the gap between them and imagine a magnet in each fingertip, pulling them together. Feel the magnetic force growing stronger – pulling, drawing them closer and closer. Watch as your fingers move toward each other. If and when they touch, blow on them, and they will come apart.

How to judge your reaction: If your fingers move together – or even feel as if they are "stuck" – it indicates a strong focus and imagination. If they remain stuck until you blow on them, it's a clear sign that your mind is highly responsive to suggestion, which is a positive indicator for hypnosis.

Light and Heavy Hands

This exercise explores the power of suggestion in using focus, imagination and visualisation to influence sensations – perfect for demonstrating the mind-body connection!

What to do: Stand or sit comfortably with your hands extended in front of you. Your right palm should facing up and your left palm facing down. Close your eyes and imagine holding a large, heavy wooden bucket in your right hand, reinforced with iron bands. Now, picture the bucket being filled with big rocks, weighing it down. Next, imagine it filling with thick, wet sand, making it even heavier.

At the same time, visualise a large, colourful bunch of helium balloons tied to your left wrist, gently but persistently pulling your hand upward. Imagine adding more balloons, feeling their lift grow stronger. As you concentrate, notice the contrast – the increasing weight in your right hand as more sand is added and the light, buoyant pull in your left as more balloons float skyward. Continue this visualisation for about a minute.

How to judge your reaction: Open your eyes. If one hand has risen and the other has lowered, you've experienced the power of suggestion. The greater the gap between your hands, the stronger your imagination – an excellent sign of your ability to respond to hypnosis and benefit from suggestion.

What Do Your Results Mean?

If you felt any of these sensations vividly, it's a positive indicator of your powers of focus, imagination and visualisation. You are likely a good hypnotic subject! Don't worry if it was subtle, or that it took time or even if nothing happened. Suggestibility is unique to everyone and often increases with practice. The keys are relaxation, openness and curiosity – qualities that naturally deepen with each hypnosis session.

We are just about ready now to do some Stabilisation hypnosis!

In this process, as in all the hypnotherapy sessions in this book, your mind will remain active and alert. You'll hear everything I say and remember as much as you would from any normal conversation. Hypnosis isn't about losing control – it's about gaining control over the parts of your life that no longer need to feel out of control.

You may experience a deep sense of relaxation, a light, floating sensation, or simply feel as though you're sitting on a chair or lying in bed. There isn't one specific way to feel when hypnotised, and whatever you experience is perfectly fine. At times, you may be fully engaged in every word I say, while at other moments, your mind might drift elsewhere. That's completely normal.

Just allow yourself to relax into the process. Hypnosis isn't something I do to you, but something we do together. It's simply a matter of following easy instructions. If I ask you to imagine something, imagine it. If I ask you to think about something, think about it. And if you ever feel the need to move, scratch or adjust, go ahead – doing so will only help you relax even more.

Before we do that, I want to be clear that your safety is my first priority. While for most people hypnosis is gentle, pleasant and extremely safe, some conditions do come with an elevated risk, so please read the hypnosis health warning in Appendix 2 before using the link to access the hypnotherapy session.

As we are in the Stabilisation phase, the focus is on letting go of what has been holding you back and taking the first steps toward reclaiming your calm, confidence and resilience. The hypnosis audios in later chapters will help you develop positive habits and traits to support this transformation.

So sit down, ideally with your head and neck supported, or lie down, and scan the code below...

I hope that you found that helpful and are already noticing a difference. For some people, the difference is immediate. For others, it can take some time as the subconscious mind processes the changes. I have had a number of clients who don't even notice the changes until someone else has pointed them out!

Keep listening to this session daily until you feel that you are ready to move on.

Havening Techniques ®

The final technique we'll explore in the Stabilisation phase is a psychosensory method known as Havening Techniques ®.

These powerful techniques are highly effective in reducing or eliminating negative feelings.

Havening, developed by Dr. Ronald Ruden, is based on the idea that therapeutic touch, eye movements and visualisation can help rewire neural pathways associated with emotional distress.[3]

The theory suggests that these techniques can boost serotonin production, a chemical known for its soothing effects on mental health. It may also stimulate delta brain waves, which are linked to deep relaxation and the brain's natural healing processes. Together, these effects help you relax and detach from distressing feelings, memories or experiences. These techniques can also boost your overall well-being and lead to improved focus and performance, so they are also good techniques in the Development phase.

In essence, this approach aims to help you create a peaceful and calm "haven" for yourself – hence the term "Havening."

There is a link to the Havening organisation website in the Resources section, if you would like to find out more.

Dealing With Anxiety

Here are two quick and simple tapping techniques – Butterfly Tapping and Single Spot Tapping – rooted in traditional Chinese medicine and acupressure. These are also part of a more advanced tapping protocol covered in the next chapter.

As mentioned earlier, anxiety can surface at any time, in any phase, or even after you've made progress. That's why each chapter will conclude with a practical technique to help you manage it effectively and quickly return to a calm state.

These techniques are not phase-specific, and different techniques work best for different people, so try them all and see which works best for you.

Butterfly Tapping

This one can be done with eyes open or closed – try both and see which feels better.

Simply cross your arms over your chest so they cross at or about the wrists, with your middle fingers pointing to the opposite shoulder and each of your thumbs touching the point of the opposite collarbone, just below your neck.

Take a deep breath in, hold it for seven counts and then gradually let it go. Allow yourself to relax as you exhale.

At a medium pace, repeatedly tap your thumbs on the point of the collarbone for up to two minutes, or until the feeling has gone, which may well happen earlier.

As you finish, say, "All is well."

If the anxiety still persists after two minutes, repeat this process until it is gone. For longer-lasting effects, you can repeat this up to three times a day.

I have also seen this called "Butterfly Hugging" and versions in which you also interlink your thumbs and tap your hands, but I find that the above approach works best.

In addition to being based on acupressure points and incorporating a psychosensory element – similar to Havening – butterfly tapping also involves some bilateral stimulation, which we explored in the "Dealing with Anxiety" section of the previous chapter.

Single Spot Tapping

There is a point at the top of your head known as the "anxiety spot," which we will be tapping.

Some people worry about finding the exact spot, but there's a simple workaround: hold the four fingers of one hand together so the tips form a straight line, then place them along the centerline of your head, running from front to back.

Take a deep breath in, hold it for a count of 7, then slowly exhale, allowing yourself to relax as you let go.

Now, tap moderately firmly (not so hard that it hurts!) and at a steady pace on the anxiety spot—about 50 times or for 3 minutes—while repeating the phrase, "Release and let it go."

For longer-lasting effects, you can repeat this practice up to three times a day, just as with Butterfly Tapping.

Chapter Recap

This was our first foray into tools and techniques that can help to stabilise us – in other words, that "restore factory settings" or "let the snow globe settle" and help overcome the thoughts, feelings and negative patterns holding us back.

We explored how you can use repetition as you "fake it 'til you make it" if you are wary of using therapy techniques such as NLP or hypnotherapy.

We looked at NLP and how by "changing the recipe" of how we "do" negative thoughts, feelings and behaviours, we can very quickly get rid of them.

We dived into hypnosis and hypnotherapy, explored what it is, addressed common questions and myths, and explained that while it is a safe and enjoyable process for most people, there are situations where it should be avoided or where medical advice should be sought before proceeding.

We had some fun with suggestibility tests that you can also try at home on friends and family, and did our first hypnotherapy session.

Chapter 6
Development

"Without continual growth and progress, such words as improvement, achievement and success have no meaning."
– Benjamin Franklin

Once you have used the tools in the previous chapter regularly and got yourself to the stage where you feel calm, relaxed and, above all, confident and ready to push on for the success that you want and believe that you deserve, it is time to really kick on and move into the Development phase of the ASDIC Framework.

This is the phase where you gain momentum, clarifying what you truly want – and, just as importantly, why you want it. Taking this step helps ensure that the success you achieve is both meaningful and fulfilling rather than a pursuit that leaves you feeling unsatisfied.

At this point, I am going to ask you to think about what I call "the magic wand question." If I could wave a magic wand and instantly give you the life, success and future you've always dreamed of, what would it look like? What would you be, have and do? Keep thinking about it as you go through this chapter.

With a nod to ensuring that your plans and goals are focused on the right thing, I regularly use the Wheel of Life with my clients. There are plenty of websites that go into this in detail. Most of these allow you to do the basics for free but then have a paywall before you can move on to more advanced aspects, so I will not dwell on it much here. Allow me to explain the basics and recommend that you do the exercise and complete the Wheel of Life before moving on to Motivation and Goal Setting.

As you will see, there are different versions of the Wheel, depending on which site you choose to look at. The wheel typically consists of between eight and ten categories of elements that should be addressed in the balance of your life. The themes of the segments are fairly standard, although the names may differ.

Here is an example of one that has 8 segments and uses a spider-web design.

THE WHEEL OF LIFE

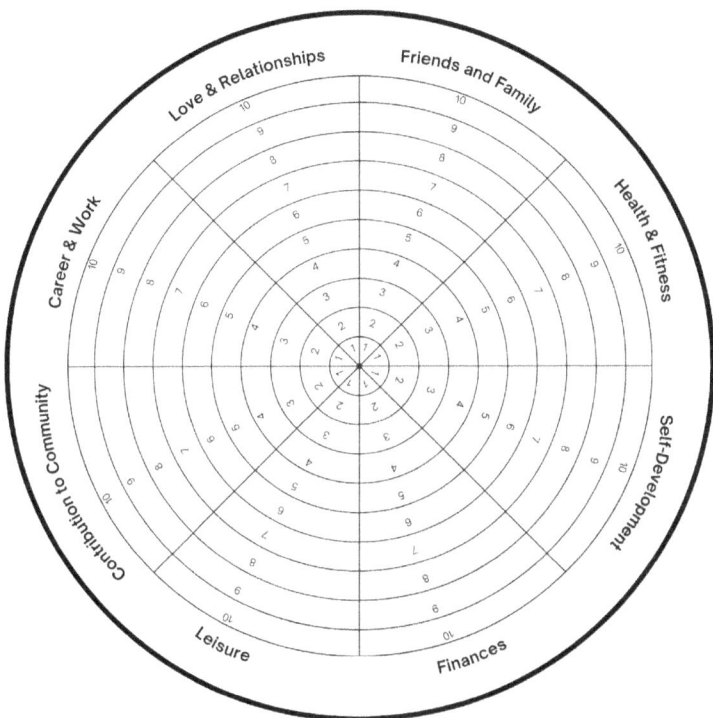

Using the Wheel is simple. Start by looking at each area in turn and rating where you feel you currently are in your life on a scale of 1 to 10 (I've just realised how often I use a 1 to 10 scale!). Here, 1 represents the lowest possible score, and 10 is perfect. Draw a circle around your chosen number in each section.

Next, take a straight edge and connect the circled numbers across the wheel, moving from one section to the next.

Now, repeat the process, this time scoring where you want to be in each area. Draw a circle around each new number and connect them as before (using a different colour if possible).

The result will be a "spider's web" that highlights your strengths, areas that need improvement and the biggest gaps between your current situation and your ideal. These insights will serve as the foundation for your goal setting, which we'll explore later in the chapter.

Before we get there, let's look at getting and staying motivated.

Motivation

Picture this: It's the final month of the year, and you receive an unexpected call from your department head. You've been selected for a career-defining opportunity – an all-expenses-paid invitation to speak at a prestigious global conference. You'll be sharing the stage with industry leaders, including your CEO. The only catch? You have just one week to prepare your presentation and be ready to fly out.

Would you seize the opportunity? Absolutely!

You'd likely dedicate every waking moment to perfecting your presentation, rehearsing your speech and ensuring you have all the necessary materials. You'd clear your schedule, delegate tasks and perhaps even pull a few late nights to make sure everything is flawless. You'd buy new clothes, carefully pack your suitcase and double-check every detail.

In just 24 hours, you'd probably accomplish more than you have in the last 24 days. The sheer importance of the opportunity would push you to perform at your absolute best.

But here's the key question: Why aren't you operating at this level of intensity and focus every day? Suddenly, you're fully productive – working at a level you've always been capable of but rarely reached.

The potential for high performance is always within you, yet it often remains dormant until a compelling reason awakens it.

This brings us back to the importance of motivation and the role of a powerful "Why." As Tony Robbins says, if the Why is big enough, you'll find the How. When the rewards are clear and big enough, your subconscious mind shifts into high gear, pushing you to achieve what you once thought was impossible.

But how do you maintain that drive once the immediate incentive fades? It boils down to consistently renewing your motivation and keeping your goals at the forefront of your mind. What's controlling that? It's not your company, it's not your boss, it's not your clients. No – it's what's going on inside your head; it's what you're focused (or not focused) on at a subconscious level.

If you accept that, then it stands to reason that if you could somehow reprogram yourself to begin focusing on a greater level of success, a greater level of productivity, more sales, more income, whatever, then your productivity in achieving these things will rise.

You'd start doing things you hadn't, and, at the end of the year, you would likely be far more successful and have achieved more simply because you changed the way you thought and focused.

Let's look at it another way by shifting to your long-term ambitions. Let's say you've cloned yourself. I then ask you and your clone, "Where do you see yourselves five years from today?" Your clone confidently responds, "My goal – what I will focus on every single day – is having £1 million in the bank." Meanwhile, the original you says, "I'm focused on maybe having a few pounds saved up."

Which version of you do you think is more likely to reach that £1 million goal, or at least be well on the way to achieving it?

What's going on between your ears has a lot to do with the way you work and the productivity you generate.

I'm sure you have heard that before, so here's the problem: motivation. Having a vision that is big enough and clear enough – and making sure your Why is big enough and clear enough for you to find the How.

It's actually very easy to get motivated. What's difficult is staying motivated. The most obvious example of that is New Year's resolutions.

The most common resolution is to lose weight. If you ask someone with that goal, "What's your motivation?" they'll likely say something like: "I'll look better. I'll feel better. I'll finally wear clothes I haven't been able to fit into for years. I'll be healthier. I'll have the confidence to go to the pool. I won't feel embarrassed on the beach when I go on holiday…"

They're filled with motivation – clear, powerful, and deeply personal reasons to succeed. Yet, nine times out of ten, just a few weeks later, they're back to indulging in sugary, unhealthy foods and drinks. So what happened?

If you're brave enough to ask them, "What about the weight you wanted to lose? What about looking better, feeling better, wearing the clothes you used to fit into, or feeling confident on the beach?" they'll likely shrug and say something like, "Life's too busy right now. There's just too much going on." The problem wasn't getting motivated – it was staying motivated.

That's the challenge with motivation. For most people, it's easy to find but hard to hold on to. In fact, motivation often lasts no more than 48 hours before it starts to fade.

Let's take a business example. How many times have you attended a conference or training session where the speakers were inspiring, the music energising and the atmosphere electric? You've been wined and dined, networked with peers and maybe even celebrated a little. You left feeling unstoppable, ready to get back to the office and smash it out of the park.

But how long did that feeling last? Be honest – probably not more than two days.

A week later, most people are right back to doing things the way they always have; the same habits, the same routines, the same levels of productivity. Sound familiar?

The problem is that motivation is very transitory. Most people can't stay motivated, and they end up going back to their default setting.

Notice how I keep saying most people – but not everybody.

Once in a while, you'll come across a person who appears to be constantly motivated, constantly pushing themselves (and sometimes you) forward. They may seem a bit wearing, as they are always on the go, trying to get you to the same level of motivation, but there's usually a nagging (and slightly envious) voice in your head asking, "How do they do that? I wish I could be that enthusiastic."

A mentor of mine – top corporate hypnotist Anthony Galie – started asking people what they did to stay motivated. Probably more than 90% responded by looking up at the ceiling, shuffling their feet, rubbing their chin and in general looking a bit confused. There would be a pause, then they'd give a very vague answer, like "Well, I try to get up at the same time every morning", "I try to get to work on work time" or "I try to keep my head down and work hard." Their answers were very vague, very nebulous.

Less than 10% hesitated, but only briefly – they were probably not used to being asked the question – coming back faster and in much greater detail. The more successful the person was, the higher up the corporate food chain they were, the faster and more detailed their reply: "What do I do to stay motivated? Well, I'll tell you…"

It quickly became clear that the more successful someone was – and the longer they had sustained that success – the faster they responded. When asked how they stayed motivated, they all answered without hesitation and in detail. They all had a strategy to stay motivated, always doing it within the 24- to 48-hour window of first feeling that spark. Most practised it daily, while others did it two or three times a week, but without fail, they took action within that critical 48-hour period – and they could tell you exactly what it was.

For most, it took less than five minutes a day to do what kept them motivated. If they didn't do it, they said they would feel as if they were losing their edge and their focus, and their performance would start to go down.

They were all running a mental program. They were repeatedly motivating themselves, starting within that 48-hour window. While many of the examples were unique, one thing came up over and over again. What do you suppose that answer was? I'm sure that you know because I mentioned it above.

Goals

Yes, "I set goals" was the most common response. As I write this, the Olympics have not long finished and I am sure that you too heard the medalists talking about how, at a young age, they had set themselves the goal, or vision, of winning an Olympic medal, and how that had driven them forward, hour by hour, day by day, week by week, month by month, year by year.

That is also a perfect example of a subconscious programme installed by repetition, as we discussed in Chapter 2.

If you set a clear vision, define your goals, write them down and affirm them regularly, you'll embed them into your subconscious – naturally guiding yourself toward them in a way you never have before.

Now, honestly, do you do it? Do you write your goals down, ideally at least 3 or 4 times a week? Preferably every day, but most especially within that first 48 hours of getting motivated.

You've probably heard about it, you very likely know it, and yet only two people out of a hundred do it. If you're in the 2%, well done, you are on the way to achieving those goals! If you are in the other 98%, why don't you do it? It's simple to do, it's free, it's easy; you don't have to attend a course, and you certainly don't have to pay anybody to do it for you. So, why not?

The most common excuse? "I'm just too busy." Really? Top performers spend just 3 to 4 minutes a day writing down or repeating their goals – yet everyone else claims they don't have the time!

If you're not keen on writing your goals down, an equally effective alternative is hearing them every day. Instead of seeing them on paper, you'll be reinforcing them through sound.

Take 30 minutes to jot down your goals, or just the key points, then record a 3- to 4-minute audio file, repeating each goal at least three times in your own voice. This creates a powerful tool: an audio reminder, spoken by you, reinforcing your goals through repetition – the key to embedding them in your subconscious. Listen to it at least once a day: in the car, during your morning coffee, at the gym, on a walk, or anytime you can fit in five minutes while doing something else.

If you do this every day for 30 days, your goals will become second nature. If I were to ask you what your goals were at the end of that month, you wouldn't look up at the ceiling, avoid eye contact and hesitate. You'd be able to recite them effortlessly, with absolute clarity – because they'd be deeply embedded in your subconscious.

Repetition has the same effect as television commercials. In fact, that's how television commercials work. They don't just play the commercial occasionally or once or twice. They'll take a commercial and play it over and over and over and over again until you know every word and every note of the "jingle" (or aural signature, as I believe it is called) unconsciously and can recall it reflexively.

Advertisers know that if they can capture your attention – even for just one second, but repeatedly – your conscious and unconscious mind will start to recognise their product. The more they reinforce that connection, the more likely you are to choose their brand over the competition.

I tried an experiment once in a course I taught. Based on an old TV commercial, I asked, "What are twicicles as nicicles?" and about half the attendees (admittedly the older half) fired back "Ricicles." Ricicles have not been sold anywhere in the world since 2017. That's the power of repetition!

So, writing your goals down is one way. Hearing them is another. There is a third way of programming yourself. Instead of seeing your goals written down or hearing them on an audio file, you can achieve the same results by visualising them.

This is not as easy as the other two and generally works best for people whose dominant Rep System is visual, and strongly so. If you listen to interviews or podcasts with highly successful people in almost any field, you'll often hear them say things like: "When I left school, I had no qualifications, little money and was living in a bedsit. I wasn't driving a beautiful car – but I had a vision, a dream. I could see myself achieving it. I drove an old car because it was all I could afford, but I taped pictures of a Mercedes to the dashboard and my bathroom mirror. I always knew I'd own one someday. My spouse and I envisioned the home we wanted, talked about it every day, and stuck pictures of it on the fridge. We used to dream about it – now we're living in it."

Even if they haven't written them down or listened to them, they were laser-focused on them, every day seeing pictures in their head or on a vision board or the like that they created, on which they put pictures of their dream home, their dream car, their dream job, their dream holiday destination. They bypassed their conscious mind and put it straight into their subconscious. Essentially, they hypnotised themselves. But deliberate self-hypnosis is a topic for another day.

That's how simple it can be to program yourself – to give your brain a pattern to follow – towards achieving your goals. Anything you hear or do repetitively becomes internal and happens unconsciously very quickly. It's like exercise; if you do it over and over, you will get results. That's a very powerful tool for you to harness, but very few people use it. Consider the daily routine of someone without clear goals. They might have a vague idea of what they'd like to accomplish, but nothing structured. They arrive at work, check emails, make a few calls and have a brief burst of activity – then they pause. Without a written plan or a clear system to follow, they hesitate: "What should I do next?" "I could do this… or maybe that… I think I'll grab a coffee."

This cycle repeats: another short burst of work, followed by another pause. Maybe they handle some paperwork, then stop again, wondering what to tackle next. By the end of the day, their productivity has been scattered, broken up by periods of indecision and inactivity (except for refilling their coffee cup), simply because their brain had no structured path to follow.

It is estimated that the average person can get 20% or more done every day if they have written goals. There's a lot of wasted time going by, and this is mainly because most people have nothing to follow.

That's why setting goals and writing, recording or visualising them can be a game-changer for you.

Setting Goals

Ok, now that we understand the impact goals have, how do we go about setting them? The most common way is to have long-term, medium-term and short-term goals.

Long-term goals. These are where you dream big. Think of the house you want to live in five or ten years from now, the car you want to drive, where you want to spend your holidays, the income that you want, the amount of money you want in the bank etc.

Medium-term goals. These span about a year to 18 months and are the actionable steps toward realising those long-term dreams.

Short-term goals. These are practical and immediate, focusing on what you want to accomplish today or this week. They often take the form of a "to-do" list, but with the principle of beginning with the end in mind, it's best to prioritise actionable steps that move you closer to your medium- and long-term goals.

As we saw earlier when we looked at the Wheel of Life, there are up to 10 key dimensions by which your life can be measured and goals set. While you can choose which of these you want to focus on and which (if any) you leave to one side, I believe that to keep balance in your life, you need to have some goals for yourself away from work, whether for relaxation or to develop a skill or passion that you have and, ideally, some community or society based goals.

In today's world, we are encouraged to focus on business and "achievement" goals. However, as humans, we are inherently social beings – wired for connection and community. It's easy to overlook this in the pursuit of success, focusing solely on productivity and measurable accomplishments and ignoring the benefits of taking time out from day-to-day madness.

There is a lot of evidence to suggest that a focus on external goals only – even if they are achieved – is likely to leave you feeling unfulfilled. This can have a massively detrimental impact on your mental health and can be a contributor to depression.

For a well-rounded life, your goals should align with the areas you explored in the Wheel of Life exercise at the beginning of this chapter. If not, at the very least, consider setting goals in the following key areas: business and career, financial, family and relationships, health, and social and community.

Key Characteristics

There are five key characteristics that life goals should have to maximise the chances of achieving them. I am sure you have work goals, which are normally set for you, but I see these as slightly different and will touch on them later in this chapter.

They Are Specific and Written Down (or Recorded)

If a goal is not specific, it is just a wish. Most people dream about "being rich." However, without specificity about what that means, it is just that – a dream. For your dream to be truly effective as a goal, it needs to be as specific as can be. For example, if your goal is financial stability, have a specific amount of income or amount in the bank (or in stock and shares if that is what you believe is part of financial stability).

Writing it down or recording it as an audio file and then revisiting it and reading it or listening to it as often as possible, at least once every 48 hours, ideally at the beginning and end of the day, will embed it into your subconscious.

The more often you repeat them, the quicker the goals will manifest.

In his book *Goals,* renowned motivational speaker Brian Tracy cites a study of Harvard MBA graduates from a few years ago.[4] Upon graduation, only 3% had written goals, 13% had goals but hadn't written them down, and 84% had no specific goals. A decade later, the 13% with unwritten goals were earning twice as much as those without any goals. But the 3% who had clear, written goals were earning, on average, ten times more than the other 97% combined.

They Are Measurable and Objective

You've likely heard the expression, "If you can't measure it, you can't manage it." The same applies to your goals and connects directly to the importance of being specific. If you don't have a clear definition of your goal, how will you know if you're making progress – or if you've already achieved it?

They Are Challenging

Achieving your goals should challenge you, but that doesn't mean they're out of reach. You should have confidence that you can acquire the skills and resources needed to succeed, but aim for goals with about a 50% probability of success. This balance helps maintain focus and motivation.

They Are Timebound

As Brian Tracy says, there are no unrealistic goals, just unrealistic timelines. A goal without a deadline is, again, just a wish.

If you have seen Tim Urban's excellent Ted Talk "Inside the Mind of a Master Procrastinator," you will be aware that a lack of deadlines is the greatest ally of the Instant Gratification Monkey (the creature in your brain that is always looking to distract you).[5] If you haven't seen it, go and watch it. If you miss a deadline, don't worry or panic. Work out why that happened and set a new, realistic one.

They Are Congruent

Your goals must be congruent with each other and with your values. If they are not, you will experience cognitive dissonance, which will need to be resolved before you can experience fulfilment.

Tips Towards Effective Goals

When writing or recording your goals, there are three main characteristics that will really help them take hold and be effective. Interestingly, they are also three of the main attributes of effective hypnotic self-suggestions.

They should be expressed in the positive. For example, "I am confident speaking in front of a room full of people" and not "I am not scared of speaking in front of a room full of people."

They should be expressed in the present tense, as if you have already achieved it. For example, "I earn £250,000 per year" and not "I will earn £250,000 per year."

They should be expressed in the first person. Every goal should start with the word "I" followed by a verb.

Work SMART Goals

You may have noticed that these principles are similar to – but not fully aligned with – the SMART (Specific, Measurable, Achievable, Relevant, Time-bound) goal-setting framework, which is widely used in corporate environments. That's intentional. SMART goals work well in a business setting, where "achievable" is often set conservatively (typically below 50%), and "relevant" means aligned with the company's broader objectives. Despite discussions about "balance," it rarely plays a meaningful role in workplace goals.

From personal experience, I also suspect that most corporate SMART goals aren't revisited every 48 hours. Instead, because they are assigned rather than personally created, they tend to be filed away – whether in a drawer or a digital folder – only to be dusted off at the next mid-year review. As you now know, this lack of frequent engagement means they don't benefit from the power of repetition, which is key to embedding goals in your subconscious and turning them into reality.

NLP

We have already looked at how you can use the NLP "submodalities" process to switch off a negative state. However, NLP doesn't just work to improve negative states. You can also use the same process to "switch on" a positive state. Here's how you do it.

Choose the positive state you would like to be in. For example, powerful, happy or peaceful. Then, think of a time or a situation when you felt that way. Breathe deeply, close your eyes and relive it. Imagine it vividly. See what you saw, hear what you heard and feel what you felt. Make the colours brighter, the sounds louder and the positive feeling even stronger.

As you achieve the peak of that positive state, do some action (pinching your thumb and forefinger together is a very common one) and hold that for a count of eight, while maintaining that peak state. This physical action is known as an "anchor", and your subconscious will associate it with that peak state. Repeat the process another two times, each time making the colours brighter and brighter, the sounds louder and the positive feeling even stronger.

Finally, test it. When you need a boost, repeat the thumb-forefinger gesture to trigger those positive emotions instantly. That should do the trick, but if you want to go a bit deeper, you can adjust all the submodalities just as you did in the previous chapter to find what "recipe" gives you the best results.

Hypnosis and Hypnotherapy

You will find the link to the hypnotherapy session for the Development phase of the ASDIC Framework below.

In this session, I work with your unconscious mind to address any past barriers, ensuring it finds new, safe and healthy ways to fulfill its positive intent – because your subconscious always acts with your best interests in mind. Then, we shift to vividly envisioning your desired future, fully aligned with your goals, and embed that vision deep into your subconscious, anchoring the feeling of achievement.

As with all the hypnosis sessions, I want to be clear that your safety is my first priority, so please read Appendix 2 carefully before using the qr code to access the hypnotherapy session.

If you are ready to go, sit down, ideally with your head and neck supported, or lie down, and scan the code on the next page to access the hypnosis audio for the Development Phase.

As with the audio for the Stabilisation phase, just keep listening to the Development session daily until you feel that you are ready to move on.

Dealing With Anxiety

I have already introduced a couple of tapping protocols for dealing with anxiety. Here, I am going to turn that up a notch and introduce 6 Spot Tapping, also known as the Emotional Freedom Technique (EFT).

As mentioned, these techniques for dealing with anxiety at the end of each chapter are not specific to the phase of the ASDIC Framework but can be used at any time. I simply want to introduce you to a number of techniques so you can try them and work out which works best for you.

6-Spot Tapping (EFT)

Ensure you're well-hydrated before starting. If not, drink some water and wait 10 minutes.

Begin by naming the feeling, such as "the anxiety" or "that tense feeling." Avoid calling it "my anxiety" or "my tense feeling," as anxiety is something you experience, not something you own or are. Next, calibrate the intensity by rating it on a scale of 0 to 10, where 0 means completely calm and 10 feels like you're about to break down.

Now, start tapping each of the following points about 12 times while repeating a phrase, such as "Let it go" or "Calm and relaxed" – whatever resonates most with you. Tap the middle of the top of your head (the "anxiety spot" from Chapter 5), the centre of your forehead, the temple beside the corner of one eye, the cheekbone directly under the pupil of the same eye and the lower side of the collarbone just off-centre (the same place used for "Butterfly Tapping" in Chapter 5). Then, tap the inside of one wrist or, even better, squeeze your wrist, while saying "Let it go."

Once you've completed the tapping sequence, take a deep breath, exhale, relax and say, "Peace, all is well." Recalibrate the intensity level, and if necessary, repeat the process until the feeling is at zero. This should take no more than five minutes. If the intensity isn't decreasing as expected, try moving to a different location, as some evidence suggests that electromagnetic waves can reduce effectiveness.

Chapter Recap

As you come out of the Stabilisation phase and are ready to step into Quadrant 4 of the 4 FU Model – Forwards & Upwards – the focus shifts to what you want to be and what you want to achieve, rather than what you want to overcome. The Wheel of Life is a useful tool to help you do this.

To move forward (and upwards!) most effectively and stay motivated, you should set effective goals. If you don't know where you are going, how will you know what direction to drive in, and, more importantly, how will you know when you get there?

There are a number of elements to creating effective goals and a number of attributes that they should have to really bring them into focus. Your goals can be embedded into your subconscious through repetition – ideally daily and certainly every two to three days. This can be done by writing them down and reading them, by recording them on an audio file and listening to them or by vividly visualising them.

As I was writing this chapter, a circular from an organisation called the Entrepreneurs Circle dropped through my letter box. On its front page was the following: "A DREAM written down becomes a GOAL. A goal broken down into steps becomes a PLAN. A plan backed by ACTION makes your dreams REALITY." Wise words!

Chapter 7
Improvement

*"Practice isn't the thing you do once you're good.
It's the thing you do that makes you good."*
– Malcolm Gladwell

*"Small daily improvements are the key to
staggering long-term results."*
– Robin Sharma

As we continue the "Forwards and Upwards" trajectory, the Development phase transitions into the Improvement phase. In this phase, we start to increase the focus on more practical aspects of becoming successful, particularly building relationships with others.

Good relationships are key to success: they can open doors and lead to better opportunities.

Good relationships can be personal or professional – ideally, both. Since this book primarily focuses on business success, I will concentrate on business relationships.

A good business relationship changes the way you think about the other person. If they fail in some way, you are inclined to blame it on external circumstances. If you don't have a relationship, you tend to put it down to malice or some other flaw in the person's nature. This works both ways – and with a good relationship, the other person is more likely to give you the benefit of the doubt if things are going wrong.

Thus, if you are likely to be in a confrontational situation with someone, start trying to build a good relationship at the earliest opportunity.

There are two key steps here. First, separate relationship issues from substantive issues. You may have heard of this as "separating the people from the problem." Build a sense of resolution as a shared challenge, of attacking a problem together (rather than attacking each other if things go wrong). Second, reason and be open to reason. Be persuaded by principle and reason, not pressure.

When you combine these with the communication approach I discuss later in this chapter, you can break down barriers and form deep and meaningful relationships. It is harder for someone to be hostile towards you if you hear them out, acknowledge their points (even if you are clear you do not agree with them) and show them respect than it would be if you have treated them with aggression, obstinacy and disrespect. You are more inclined to listen to someone who has listened to you. You are more inclined to respect someone who has given you respect.

To my mind, a good business relationship is characterised by the ability to deal well and constructively with the other person in general, yes, but particularly on substantive issues. It is not necessarily about sharing values or even liking each other – it's about dealing with each other positively and constructively.

In other words – and this can come as a shock to many people – a good business relationship is a function of behaviour, not personality. That doesn't mean you cannot also have a good personal relationship based on shared values and liking each other, but this is not a pre-requisite.

Over the years in my training courses, I have asked many executives what they think the most important aspects of a strong business relationship are and, by far, the three most common answers have been rapport, trust and communication. So, let's look at these in turn.

Rapport

Normally in society, when we build rapport with someone, it's because we have something in common with them – your school, your background, your hobbies and interests, your religion etc. If you look at your group of close friends, you'll probably find that you have something in common with all of them

And that's fine for friendships, but in business, we often have to build rapport (and quickly) with someone we don't know and with whom we have nothing in common – maybe a client, a supplier or even a colleague or boss.

As I'm sure most of you know, this is quite hard to do.

This is where an understanding of some elements of NLP comes in. Even if we have nothing in common, we all share a common "operating system" in our heads, and we can tap into that.

As we noted in earlier chapters, in most situations, including interactions with others, the first thing our unconscious mind does is scan for threats. When there is none, the next thing it looks for is touch points to help it understand the other person, with feelings of trust, safety and security increasing the greater the number of familiar traits it recognises.

Normally, the person that we trust the most and feel the most safe and secure with is the person we look at in the mirror every day: ourselves. The more like us someone is, the more "familiar touch points" they have, and the more we will feel comfortable, trusting, safe and secure with them.

At the same time, as humans, we are hardwired to fit in and mirror those around us. Imitation is a fundamental pattern of human behaviour. Observe any group, and you'll notice that if one person does something – whether it's scratching their head, folding their arms or coughing – many others will unconsciously follow. Think about how often you've been in a cinema where one person's cough sets off a chain reaction throughout the audience.

As Mark Twain said, "We are creatures of outside influence: as a rule, we do not think, we only imitate."[6]

More recently, NLP founders Richard Bandler and John Grinder studied the unconscious imitative patterns that occur between people, particularly when these patterns happen continuously. They believe this reflects true rapport – something far more specific than the general, softer concept often associated with the term. In this book, I use "rapport" in that precise sense: a noticeable sameness between two or more people that makes them subconsciously feel alike, fostering a sense of comfort and security.

I often reference *Healing: Beyond Pills & Potions* by Dr. Steve Bierman, and for good reason. In that book, he discusses building rapport – using the very techniques I'm about to explore – with patients in A&E, demonstrating how this connection can serve as the foundation for remarkable therapeutic outcomes.

So how does he – and how do we – tap into that quickly?

Bandler and Grinder looked at that as well and came up with two concepts: Mirroring and Matching, and Pacing and Leading.[7]

Mirroring and Matching

In mirroring and matching, we reflect the other person's behaviours, particularly their physical movements and voice.

The former includes actual movements like arm and hand movements, head tilts, leg crossing and uncrossing and shifting position, as well as more subtle ones like breathing and eye blinks. These need not be exact imitations or made at exactly the same time but should be similar and in a reasonably short time period after the original.

Similarly, when it comes to voice, the more that you can match the speed, cadence and volume of the other person's speech, the quicker they will become relaxed and confident in your company, and the quicker rapport will be established.

Pacing and Leading

Pacing involves mirroring and matching the physical movements and vocal qualities of the other person, allowing rapport to be built quickly. Once rapport is established, you can move to leading. This is when you introduce a movement the other person hasn't made, and they unconsciously mirror or match it back. For example, if you cross your legs and, moments later, they do the same, it signals a deepened level of connection. At this point, rapport is at its strongest, and because you are leading, your persuasive influence is significantly amplified. I know of a sales trainer who always advised clients, "Don't try to close the sale until you are in rapport and leading."

A word of caution: rapport and leading are not unidirectional! Even if you choose not to use them, you need to be aware that they could be happening to you.

I have been asked before if this counts as underhand, manipulative or unethical. I have thought about this, and I am comfortable with it as an approach for two reasons.

First, this technique simply leverages elements of human nature. There is nothing illegal about it; you don't even need to go on the dark web to find it. Anyone can learn and apply it. Those familiar with NLP are already well aware of its principles. The fact that you have invested time and effort in understanding it, while others may not have, should not be seen as an unfair advantage. It is a tool, but it cannot force anyone to act against their will.

A useful analogy can be found in Robert Cialdini's bestselling book *Influence: The Psychology of Persuasion* (often referred to as the salesman's bible). In it, he identifies seven psychological triggers that can be used to persuade people.[8] Many of these, such as scarcity or FOMO (fear of missing out), are widely employed in mainstream marketing, advertising and sales.

Second, as I mentioned, the "imitation" aspect is natural and will happen anyway, even if it is at an unconscious level for both people. I think it is better to be aware of it and use it or not use it as you see fit.

Rapport can be deepened even further, and your communication made significantly more effective, by aligning with a person's dominant representational system – the way they primarily process information.

Using Rep Systems

As you may recall from when we looked at Rep Systems, we think and process information in five representation systems that coincide with our senses: Visual, Auditory, Kinaesthetic, Olfactory (smell) and Gustatory (taste). We primarily use three of these: Visual, Auditory, and Kinaesthetic (commonly referred to as VAK).

Within those systems, each of us has preferences, and one Rep System will be dominant (though this can change depending on context). We each express ourselves best in our dominant Rep System and will be much more able to understand and relate to someone who communicates using that system.

For example, if you ask a person whose primary Rep System is Visual if they "see your point of view," they will be open to you because, subconsciously, you're speaking their language. However, asking an Auditory person the same question might create some disconnect as they'll find it harder to relate to. Instead, you'd want to use auditory phrases like "How does that sound?" or "Do you hear what I'm saying?" to build rapport more effectively.

In short, you tend to get along with people who have (or communicate in) the same dominant Rep System as you do and may struggle with people who don't, even if you can't quite put your finger on why. See what I did there?

So, if it appears you have nothing in common with someone, consider VAK as a tool for finding common ground.

How to Find the Dominant Rep System

OK, so how do you figure out which Rep System is dominant for you, and how do you identify it in others?

In my courses, I typically share the story of my house-buying experience several years ago. My wife and I saw many houses, but we narrowed it down to three. I'll describe each and ask which house you would have chosen.

In the first house, we were struck by the brightness and the quality of light pouring through the large windows, particularly the stained glass window on the landing. Stepping into the kitchen, we were greeted by a stunning view of the garden, bursting with vibrant colours and lush greenery. Each room was thoughtfully decorated in tasteful colours and shades. As we said, we could certainly see ourselves living there.

In the second house, we were immediately struck by the peaceful silence as soon as we stepped through the door. As we walked across the wooden floor, our footsteps echoed softly, adding to the stillness. As we entered the kitchen, the gentle sound of birdsong drifted in from the garden, and it felt as if the house, the garden, and the birds were calling to us, welcoming us in.

The third house felt like home the moment we walked inside. Warmth wrapped around us like a hug, and as we ran our hands over the solid stone and woodwork, we could almost feel the history and permanence of the place. There was an undeniable sense of calm and happiness within its walls. We looked at each other and said, "This feels like home."

Which house would you have chosen?

As you probably guessed, they are all the same house, but described in different Rep Systems. If you chose the first, you're likely dominant in visual. The second suggests auditory dominance and the third points to a kinaesthetic preference.

When it comes to identifying other peoples' Rep Systems, there are two main indicators: how their eyes move as they think and the language that they use.

When a person is thinking, their eye movements can reveal their dominant representational system. Looking up typically indicates they are accessing visual thoughts or memories. Looking to the sides suggests they are engaging with auditory thoughts or recollections. When they look down to their right (for right-handed individuals), they are likely accessing kinaesthetic thoughts or memories, connecting with feelings or physical sensations. Looking down to their left often indicates internal dialogue or a logical, structured thought process (known as Auditory Digital), or they may be mentally debating or deciding which representational system to use.

In addition to using these eye-accessing cues to tell what Rep System a person is using, you can also use it to tell whether they are recalling or constructing something – that is, making it up, either because they are thinking of the future or inventing, let's just say, a different version of the past. For a right-handed person, eye movements to their left typically indicate they are recalling something from memory. If their eyes move to their right, they are likely constructing or creating something.

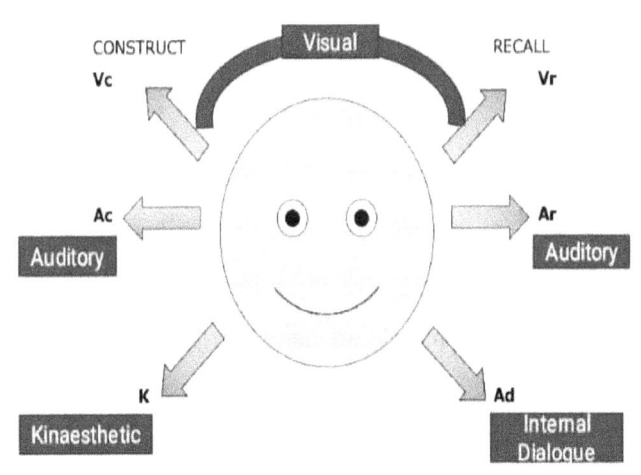

The language someone uses is also a strong indicator of their Rep System. For example, visual people often use phrases like "I can see that," "Can you picture that?" or "I'll give you an overview."

Auditory people tend to say things like "I hear you," "That sounds good," or "That rings a bell."

Kinaesthetic people might say "That feels right," "I can't put my finger on it," or "We're warming up," or talk about "getting a grip on things."

For best results, start observing someone's Rep System as soon as you meet them – even before anything formal begins. This helps you tailor your communication style right from the start. If you want to practice, watch interviews with politicians or footballers. They're great examples of Rep Systems in action! If you want to have some fun, try changing the language that you use between Rep Systems while chatting with someone and see how they react.

Trust

Trust is the key that unlocks so many things.

While much has been written on this topic and many approaches put forward as to how you can "measure" trust, my favourite, by a distance, is the Trust Equation introduced by John Maister in his Book *The Trusted Advisor*.

This says that: (Credibility + Reliability + Intimacy) divided by Self-Orientation = Trust.[9]

In the version of this that I have evolved when explaining it, I try to keep it simple.

Credibility. This is the technical expertise that enables you to do what you say you will do and your ability to demonstrate that honestly and believably. This is usually the easiest and quickest element to establish.

Reliability. This is your ability to follow through on commitments: doing what you said you would, how you said you would and when you said you would. It's about being dependable and consistent, ensuring that others can rely on you to deliver on your promises.

Intimacy. This is knowing and understanding the other person and their business deeply, inside and out, and using that to help them. It is about being able to talk openly about difficult topics.

Self-Orientation. This is the extent to which you are preoccupied with your own agenda and put that ahead of the interests or concerns of the other person. It includes anything that gives the appearance that you are more interested in yourself and your interests than the other person and theirs. For example, jumping in while the other person is speaking to give your view or offering a solution before you have heard them out and understood them and what they are trying to achieve.

So those are the elements. Now for the numbers.

We will rate each element on a scale of 1 to 10 (low to high). Stating the obvious, new relationships will produce lower numbers than existing ones: Scores should improve over time, as the understanding of how each person performs on each of the elements develops over time.

Let me use the example of a potential client.

When using the equation to try and establish how much they trust you, you might rate the client's initial perception of your credibility as a 6 (above average) on a scale of 1 to 10, based on your reputation in the marketplace. Reliability, which typically takes longer to establish, might be somewhere around 3, and Intimacy, which would not be far along at that point, might be a 3. To the other person, your Self-Orientation would score high since, as you are in a sales situation, they would typically believe that you are looking only after yourself. Thus, Self-Orientation might score an 8.

The equation, therefore, looks like this: [Credibility (6) + Reliability (3) + Intimacy (3)] divided by Self-Orientation (8) = 1.5.

So, as with most new clients, you have lots of work to do in the trust area.

With existing relationships, the score usually looks more like this: [Credibility (7) + Reliability (8) + Intimacy (5)] divided by Self-Orientation (4) = 5.

Perfection would be a score of 30. It is highly unlikely that you will ever get there, though that doesn't mean you shouldn't try.

In my view, a more realistic goal is between 12 and 20. As the relationship evolves, keep the trust score under regular review.

As with most aspects of a good relationship, your attention has to start by focusing on your own behaviour – after all, the only person you can control is you. Before you start to ask yourself whether you trust the other person, ask yourself, "Am I acting in a trustworthy manner?" This is particularly important in relation to your Self-Orientation. While trust may be built in inches, it is lost in miles, and when it is, that is usually because of a high Self-Orientation score.

Communication

I recognise that communication is a massive topic, and I will not be able to do justice to it in a part of a chapter – so I will share here some insights and tips and tricks that I have picked up and used over the years.

Ultimately, successful communication occurs when each person clearly, completely and efficiently conveys their thoughts and feels confident that they have been understood by others.

One of my favourite quotes is attributed to Pierre Martineau: "The greatest enemy of communication is the illusion of it."[10]

In my courses, I divide participants into teams and give them a word – often Trust, since it ties into our discussion, though industry-specific words work well too. Their task is to list as many synonyms as possible in two minutes.

At the end of the exercise, most teams come up with at least 15 words, sometimes far more. When I ask them to estimate how many words will appear on every team's list, the usual guess is around 10.

In reality, the overlap has never been more than two.

This simple exercise highlights just how much we need to refine our communication if we want it to be truly effective.

The truth is that you can't not communicate. Even if you are not speaking, you are communicating. That is clearly illustrated in the 7-38-55 Communication Model.

The 7-38-55 Communication Model

You may have heard of the 7-38-55 communication model, also known as the 7%-38%-55% Rule, created by Albert Mehrabian, Professor Emeritus of Psychology at the University of California Los Angeles (UCLA).

This says that when you are communicating with someone, your feelings and attitude are conveyed by how you look (55%), how you sound (38%) and what you say (7%).[11]

As a former boss of mine used to say, "Who you are being when you are saying what you are saying says more about what you're saying than what you're saying."

The 7-38-55 model is often misrepresented as being applicable to all communication, but its true significance lies in highlighting how much people rely on tone and facial expression when interpreting messages, especially when words are ambiguous or unclear. As we have just seen, misunderstandings in language are common. When there is an inconsistency between what is said and how it is said, listeners are more likely to trust the speaker's tone and body language over the literal meaning of their words.

Congruence in all three aspects is, therefore, very important.

As you know, communication has two principal dimensions: communicating with the other person and receiving communication from the other person.

Given that the only person you can control is you, you need to feel an onus both to make sure you are understood and to listen actively to make sure that you understand. Remember that it is not the other person's job to get you; it is your job to be understood.

Listening

Listening well and actively is arguably the much harder skill to master and takes time and practice, so we'll look at that first.

Why is it harder? Generally, we are all very poor listeners. In a conversation or discussion, most people either listen only partially, then their mind wanders off and they start thinking about how they are going to respond (or about something else entirely!), or they listen only so they can tell the other person they're wrong, criticise them or so they can defend their own view.

When you are doing that, how can you be listening?

So when you have "listened" in that way and made the point you were mulling over while the other person was talking, the other person thinks, "Hey, they didn't address my point. They can't have heard me. I'd better repeat it – only this time, louder."

For your thoughts to turn quickly to your own views and opinions, particularly in a contentious or charged situation, is completely normal. In such a situation, people are suspicious of the motives of others and are looking for their worst fears to be confirmed. While a natural reaction, it is neither helpful nor conducive to full, open and constructive communication. For this reason, active listening is key.

Active listening requires complete focus on the speaker, aiming to understand not just their words but also their underlying meaning and any unspoken messages. It involves listening to comprehend rather than to criticise or defend. True active listening is accepting and non-judgemental, prioritising understanding over reaction. It also means asking clarifying questions before advocating your own perspective or defending your position.

So, the first thing we need to focus on is listening for the purpose of understanding. Understanding someone and letting them know you understand them does *not* mean agreeing with them!

It means being interested, not interesting. Listen to them.

It means playing what they have said back to them to make sure you have understood it. If you think of the most important conversations you have outside of work – like asking for directions, or, if you are a climber, checking that someone is on belay before you commit your life to the mountain face – you always repeat back what they have said to confirm it. Adopt that approach in your important business conversations!

This will help you develop one of the fundamental abilities of a truly successful communicator – the ability to put yourself in another person's shoes and understand their point of view, even if you don't agree with it. When you do that, they will feel heard. Once the other person feels they have been heard and that you understand, they will feel much more relaxed and, in turn, be less defensive and more open to listening to what you have to say.

If you want to practice, try this.

Next time you are in a discussion about something important, listen with your full attention. Be interested and curious. Listen with your full attention, putting aside your own thoughts. Force yourself not to say anything other than "Tell me more about that" or "Help me understand that," or paraphrase back to them what they have just said to you.

Notice how different that felt – and how difficult it was not to start giving your point of view. Notice also the reaction of the speaker and how their attitude and reaction towards you differ from what you normally experience!

Practise that regularly. Once you are comfortable at that level, take it up a notch and start looking for what is not said. What does their tone of voice say? What does their facial expression say? What words are they not saying that you might expect? Do your very best to remain silent. If you have to speak, the same rules apply as previously.

As with all things, practice, practice, practice – and you will be amazed at the changes this brings to the clarity and effectiveness of your communication

Communicating Out

The other side of communication is expressing your thoughts outwardly – communicating out – generally through speaking or writing. While many elements apply to both, written communication – particularly in emails and messages – carries a higher risk of miscommunication as there is no real vocal tone or body language to guide the message. A discussion of that would warrant an entire chapter, if not a whole other book.

The most basic rule when it comes to talking to another person is to think about what they hear, not what you say. Put yourself in their shoes. As with listening, this is a key skill. Don't just think about how what you are saying sounds to you; think about how it sounds to them. Will they take your statements as dismissive, challenging or offensive – even if that is not your intent? Remember, the best feedback on how well you are communicating is the reaction that you get from the other person!

Follow These Guidelines for Communicating Out

Listen actively, and let them know you are listening. Pay close attention to what they say in order to understand things as they do. Do not confuse empathy with agreement. Demonstrate your attentiveness by inquiring. Ask clarifying questions like "Am I correct in understanding you are saying...?" or "What do you hear me saying?" Press them to clarify any ambiguities. Repeat back to them what you've heard to check its accuracy.

Speak for a purpose. Before making a significant statement, know what you want to communicate or find out and what purpose this information will serve.

Don't grandstand. Keep private channels of communication open. Most decisions are made by two people having an open and honest conversation, not by an audience!

Speak for yourself, not the other person. Where possible, talk about what you have observed or felt. Avoid attributing motives to the other person – you cannot know for sure what they intended, only the impact of their actions on you. Avoid telling the other person what they meant or what they think. You can only be sure of how you heard it and how you felt.

Avoid ad hominem attacks. When you start attacking the person rather than the topic of discussion, you have lost control of the conversation. At the same time, don't take it as a personal attack if the other person criticises your opinion.

Avoid or defuse the "toxic behaviours." As identified by John Gottman, these behaviours are blame, defensiveness, stonewalling and contempt.[12] If you find yourself engaging in or being tempted to engage in any of these behaviours, stop and take time to recentre yourself. If the person with whom you are communicating starts engaging in these behaviours, do not respond in kind. If you do, you are letting your emotions hijack you and the conversation. Either try to reframe the discussion to bring it back to the topic or disengage. Nothing good will come of continuing a conversation where these behaviours are being exhibited. In the words often attributed to Ambrose Bierce (although not included in any of his published work): "Speak when you are angry and you'll make the best speech that you'll ever regret."

Avoid mandates. Use language that reduces or avoids resistance. Instead of telling someone they "need to," "must," or "will" do something, use more open-ended and flexible phrasing.

- **Use permissive language.** Phrases like "You can…," "You could…," or "You might…" offer choices rather than commands.

- **Use indirect suggestions.** Try phrases such as "I wonder if…" or "Imagine with me that you did something different." Another approach is "I don't need to tell you…" (which avoids triggering resistance like "Well, actually, you do need to tell me!").

- **Use attributed quotes.** Introduce an idea by attributing it to someone else, e.g., "Many people have said…" or "I had someone tell me just the other day that when they did this, that happened."

- **Use metaphors or stories.** Whether fact or fiction, stories can be powerful tools for conveying meaning. They allow the listener to interpret the message in a way that resonates with them personally.

NLP

In the Improvement Phase, you can use the same NLP process as in the Development Phase to "switch on" a positive state. Here's a recap of how you do it.

To create a strong positive emotional state, start by choosing the feeling you want to experience – whether it's confidence, happiness or calmness. Recall a specific time when you truly felt that way, then close your eyes, take deep breaths, and immerse yourself in the memory. Visualise it vividly – enhancing the colours, amplifying the sounds and intensifying the emotions.

At the peak of this positive state, establish a physical "anchor" by performing a small action, such as pinching your thumb and forefinger together, and hold it for a count of eight. This links the gesture to the emotional state in your subconscious. Repeat this process at least twice more, each time making the sensations even stronger.

Once set, you can test your anchor. Whenever you need an emotional boost, simply repeat the gesture, and your mind will automatically trigger the same positive feelings, helping you shift your state instantly.

If you want to go a bit deeper, you can adjust all the submodalities, just as you did in Chapter 5, to find what "recipe" gives you the best results.

Hypnosis and Hypnotherapy

You will find the link to the hypnotherapy session for the Improvement Phase of the ASDIC Framework below.

In this session, we'll focus more on the future you want and the mindset that will get you there. You'll picture yourself having already achieved your goal – really feeling what that success is like – so your subconscious starts to lock it in. The more vividly you imagine it, the more natural and achievable it becomes.

As with all the hypnosis sessions, before you go into the session, I want to be clear that your safety is my first priority, so please read Appendix 2 carefully before using the code to access the hypnotherapy session.

Ok, assuming that you have read Appendix 2 and are ready to go, sit down, ideally with your head and neck supported, or lie down, and scan the code to the hypnosis audio for the Improvement phase.

As with the audio for the Development phase, just keep listening to the improvement session daily until you feel you are ready to move on.

Dealing With Anxiety

This Chapter's technique for dealing with anxiety is very simple and very effective.

It can be summed up in the words of the Australian band Men at Work in their hit song Down Under: a "slack jaw and not much to say."

That's it. Just let your jaw go completely slack and fall open. Don't try to speak; just focus on your breathing. Take long, slow breaths in through your nose and out through your mouth, exhaling for longer than you inhale.

This is another iteration of the mind-body connection, or in this case, the body-mind connection. While jaw tensing is a stress or anxiety response, a slack jaw is a relaxation response. Noticing this and believing you are in a relaxed state because your body is showing signs of relaxation, your vagus nerve activates your parasympathetic nervous system, which turns down the flight, fight, freeze response and causes the relaxation that you were simulating to actually occur.

Chapter Recap

Good relationships are key to unlocking opportunities that help you fulfil your potential.

There are three main aspects to a good relationship: rapport, trust and communication.

You can quickly build rapport, even with someone you don't know, by first using mirroring and matching and then moving to pacing and leading.

Understand the Trust Equation to evaluate trust:

Trust = (Credibility + Reliability + Intimacy) divided by Self-Orientation.

Communication has two elements: communication in and communication out (primarily, listening and talking).

Active listening is listening completely to what is being said, as well as to what is not being said. This is a skill that greatly enhances communication but needs to be practised.

After someone has spoken (and you have been actively listening), play back to them what they have said to make sure you understand. Understanding it does not mean agreeing with it!

When communicating out (talking to someone), speak for yourself, not the other person. Avoid telling the other person what they meant or what they think. You can only be sure of how you heard it and how you felt.

Do not fall into a negative pattern of ad hominem attacks or toxic behaviours.

Use words and language patterns, such as permissive language or metaphors, that overcome or avoid resistance.

There are many things you can do to improve your relationships. Become more aware of your own behaviour (and the behaviour of others, if you are mirroring and matching) and keep practising. You will not get it right consistently at first, but as you keep working on it, you will open up new neural pathways. One day, you will suddenly realise that you are doing them naturally and reaping the benefits without even thinking about it.

Chapter 8
Consistency

*"Success doesn't come from what you do occasionally,
it comes from what you do consistently."*
- Unknown

Now that you have progressed from Stabilisation through Development and Improvement, it is time to start applying the techniques, thought patterns and behaviours you have learned regularly and consistently.

Use the tools you now have at your disposal whenever possible (and appropriate in the circumstances!). Keep practising the harder skills, such as active listening or putting yourself in the other person's shoes, until they are internalised. Keep checking in on your goals and listening to the hypnosis audios regularly, if not daily.

Some days will be easy; other days will be tough. At times, it may feel tempting to slip back into old habits. Unexpected challenges – a frustrated boss, a difficult client or a colleague looking out for their own interests – can throw you off balance. Along with building consistency in your new behavior, you'll also need to strengthen your resilience because you will be tested.

In this chapter, we'll look at a few things that can help you build consistency, including ways to deal with things that can throw you off balance and make you revert to the old ways – the most common of which is dealing with difficult people or difficult situations. Knowing ways in which you can deal with such situations is, therefore, another key skill you can develop.

Many of the communication skills we looked at in the previous chapter can help here, so make sure you do not get so flustered that you forget these – particularly avoiding toxic behaviors, building rapport, adopting a frame of mind of understanding and using language that avoids resistance. However, on some occasions, these may not be enough.

As I have said a number of times, the only person you can control is you – and the only person whose behaviour you can change is you. So, when you are confronted with a difficult person, don't think about how you can change them or fall into the defensive mode of thinking, "This person needs to change." Ask yourself, "How may I be contributing to this situation?" and "What could I change in myself and the way I speak and respond to them that may change the dynamic between us?"

While it's true that the only person whose behaviour you can change is you, you can do your best to create an environment that encourages or enables them to change.

The first thing to do is think about how you react when someone demonstrates "difficult" behaviour. Do you become defensive? Do you fight fire with fire and behave in a way that is equally difficult or combative? Do you "roll over" and give them what they want to avoid confrontation, or just keep your head down to get the encounter over with as quickly as possible?

Put Yourself in the Other Person's Shoes

When we discussed communication in the previous chapter, we mentioned the key skill of being able to put yourself in the other person's shoes. Now is the time to test that.

Imagine stepping into the other person's shoes – seeing yourself through their eyes and hearing yourself through their ears as you act in the ways identified in the previous exercise. Pay attention to how this makes you (as them) feel and how you might respond. If you (as yourself) were defensive and met aggression with aggression, you (as them) would likely become even more combative. On the other hand, if you simply gave in, they might see their behaviour as an effective tactic and continue using it to get their way.

This exercise can be even more effective if you can role-play it with a supportive friend or colleague. Brief your friend or colleague on how the person and their "difficult" behaviour makes you feel and react. This person then plays the role of you, while you step into the role and persona of the difficult person. Don't hold back! You may well get insights that you didn't have before – even into why they are behaving that way. If you can get a second colleague or friend to act as an observer and give feedback on what they observe, so much the better. A neutral person's observations are often eye-opening.

Once you have gone through this, with or without role-playing, you can get an insight into how your behaviour is contributing to the problem and creating a vicious (downward) cycle.

Now that you have realised you may well be contributing to the problem, if you could change your response, it might encourage different behaviour in the other person – behaviour that you can deal with and maintain your consistency. How do you do that?

First of all, remember that your initial reaction is just your subconscious mind following a pattern. It is just an emotional habit, so step back and take a second. Don't let your emotions hijack you; instead, consciously *choose* how you will react. There is nothing wrong with reacting in any particular way, even emotionally. But if you do, that should be a choice you have made rather than just your subconscious mind taking control. If your emotions have taken control, and you react instinctively, your conscious mind has lost control of the situation for you.

Before you respond, stop, take a breath, and think about what is going on. Formulate an appropriate response before proceeding.

When I am put in a situation where I feel that my emotions are ready to hijack me and take control, I take a pause, take my glasses off and polish them. This gives me time to restore my emotional balance and choose my response.

As I formulate a response that is appropriate while cleaning my glasses, I try to do three things: First, I put myself in the position of a neutral observer – also known as "going to the balcony" – to see what is going on. Second, I separate the impact of the way they have behaved or what they have said from their intent (putting myself in their shoes again). Lastly, I try not to take any criticism of my point of view as a criticism of me or my worth.

While there are an almost endless series of behaviours that can make people difficult, the most common are getting angry or emotional; taking, and digging in on, a position; and using threats. The most common instinctive reactions to these are getting angry or emotional (reacting in kind); rejecting their view or telling them why they are wrong (taking a position as well); and using threats back, thereby escalating the situation.

The preferred and potentially game-changing reactions that you can choose are as follows.

If the person is getting angry or emotional, diagnose what is going on. Use the "going to the balcony" technique; acknowledge that they are emotional and think about how to deal with that.

If the person is taking and digging in on a position, explore why they believe that this is appropriate. Start an open discussion around them using the communication skills learned in the previous chapter.

If the person is using threats, openly examine the consequences of the threats, particularly on them. Try to start an open discussion.

If you're finding it hard to grasp what's going on or struggling to understand or accept the other person's position, a few key concepts from the world of negotiation can help. It's worth putting in the effort to work through these, as people are rarely difficult just for the sake of it.

Don't let the term "negotiation" frighten you in this context. Just think of negotiation as "communication for the purpose of influence." When you look at it in that light, you realise that we all negotiate every day, in almost every conversation at work or at home!

Using Negotiation Concepts: Positions vs. Interests

The first concept in dealing with these situations is that of interests – working to understand what the other person's interests are.

The traditional approach to negotiation – and the approach adopted by most "difficult people" in any discussion – is very much based on trying to get their way by overpowering the other person. This is known as a "positional" approach; each person has their "position" – the outcome that they think will be best (usually decided without thought as to what the other person might want) and tries to stick to it at all costs.

This approach is far from optimal as the "difficult" person usually approaches the situation aggressively to try and bully their way to what they want. As noted above, most people respond to this style of approach by either avoiding, pushing back, rolling over and giving in (and feeling hurt) or responding in kind. This gives birth to a circle of mistrust and bad behaviour.

However, there is another approach that I believe is better and helps you continue to build consistency in your new ways. It is known as an Interests-Based approach.

The Interests-Based Approach

The Interests-Based Approach is based very strongly on the seminal books *Getting to Yes* by Roger Fisher and Bill Ury, *Getting Past No* by William Ury and the work of the Harvard Negotiation Project, as further evolved by my friends and former partners at CMI Concord, Chuck Barker and Paul Cramer.[13, 14]

It tries to make negotiation a task of jointly finding a solution that works well for everyone – a "win/win" solution. It can be seen as hard on the "problem," focused on the process, but easy on the people. While I will not go into all the aspects of this approach to negotiations here (a more in-depth introduction to it is included as a Bonus Chapter), the interests element can be the key to unlocking a positive discussion with a difficult person or a difficult discussion.

As mentioned above, a position is usually the conclusion that a person thinks will be best, usually decided by them in advance and without thought as to what the other person might want. In the positional approach, people can appear to be difficult as they tend to present and defend their position, often backed up by actual or implied threats and statements of what they will and will not do.

Positions are really the answers to the question of "What" the person wants, but in looking only at the What, the Why is overlooked or ignored.

Interests, on the other hand, are answers to why a party wants what it is asking for. They are the needs, concerns, goals, hopes and fears that underlie the person's positions.

Initially, people often struggle with the distinction between positions and interests. I know that I did, until I heard the story of the orange. This was introduced in *Getting to Yes* and was a lightbulb moment for me. What follows is my version of it.

It's a lazy Sunday afternoon, and I'm watching the football when a commotion erupts from the kitchen. I get up to investigate and find my two sons locked in a standoff, each gripping the last orange in the fruit bowl.

The shouting escalates.

"Give me that orange!"

"No, I need it!"

"I said, give it to me!"

"No way – we don't always have to do what *you* want!"

Tension is rising, and I can sense that violence is imminent. I head to the drawer, pull out the biggest knife I can find, and – after briefly reconsidering my life choices – turn my attention to the orange.

What would you do?

Like any fair parent, I slice it in half and hand each of them their share, satisfied that I've solved the problem.

But then I watch in disbelief as my younger son peels his half, tosses the fruit into the bin, and walks off with just the peel. He needed it for the muffins he was baking for the school fundraiser. Meanwhile, my older son does the exact opposite, throwing away the peel and eating only the fruit because he was simply hungry.

At that moment, it hits me: If I had just asked why they each wanted the orange, I could have given one the peel and the other the fruit – completely satisfying both of them. Instead, by assuming a simple split was the fairest solution, I ended up wasting half of what each truly needed.

Similar scenarios play out in discussions (and negotiations) every day, as people battle over positions and ignore interests, leaving possible solutions undiscovered and an escalating cycle of resentment, aggression and distrust.

A good outcome from any difficult discussion, particularly with a difficult person, is one that satisfies both people's interests as well as possible. When used skillfully, it is often possible to satisfy your interests or those of the other person, even if you don't get each other's position.

To use interests well and stop a difficult person from throwing your quest for consistency off track, here are some tips.

Work on getting an understanding of the other person's interests and their relative priority. As with so many things, putting yourself completely in the other party's shoes is probably the single most important skill in this.

Work out as best you can what your own interests are and prioritise them. Be aware that they may change and evolve over time.

The more that you can find out what motivates the other person, the better your chances of transforming the conversation or relationship from a difficult one to a positive one. Start by setting out what you assume about them and their priority. Seek to validate and revise these during your discussions with them. Talk about interests explicitly. Ask them open questions, and ask as many forms of "why" questions as you can think of for the best information. Don't be afraid to challenge them on their own interests – they may not even have thought about them. This will require patience, persistence and building trust. You should be prepared to talk about some of your interests up front. If you're not willing to tell them something about your own needs, desires, concerns and fears, then you can't expect them to be willing to talk about theirs. You may just find that when the other person sees you approaching things in this non-confrontational way, they will gladly follow!

Look for areas where yours and their interests overlap. If you can reach a consensus on something good for both of you early on, it sets a good tone for the rest of the discussion

Although positions can often look irreconcilable, once you dig into and develop an understanding of the interests, you may find that the differences are less than they first seemed. You likely have more in common than you first thought.

Once you understand the other person's interests as well as your own, you have much more scope to look at different approaches or options for meeting them, which can lead to a much more productive and positive discussion and relationship.

Using Negotiation Concepts: The Ladder of Inference

The second concept from the world of negotiation is the "Ladder of Inference." This looks at how two people can draw very different conclusions from the same set of data and how they can start to reconcile them.

The concept is grounded in what we looked at way back at the beginning of the book, namely that our brains love recognising and following patterns. When we are presented with data (which can be in many forms), our mind wants to make sense of it. So it starts looking for something similar to what it has seen before. This could be based on many things, such as past experiences or memories, suggestions from an authority figure or repetition.

The mind quickly selects data that closely matches what it has encountered before and instantly begins forming a pattern. In the blink of an eye, it filters the information, assigns meaning, draws a conclusion and solidifies a belief that this conclusion is correct.

While this can be useful in many situations, it also has significant limitations. It tends to ignore or dismiss information that doesn't fit the expected pattern, relies on potentially flawed memories of past experiences and is influenced by confirmation bias. It reinforces existing beliefs and rejects alternative perspectives.

Another issue is that different people bring their unique experiences and subconscious patterns to the same data. Although their mind will follow the same process, they can very easily come to different conclusions and beliefs.

This can be presented like this:

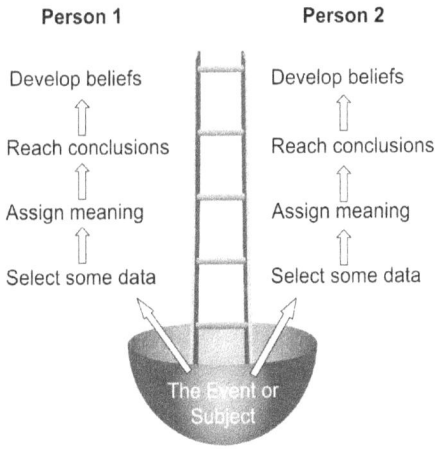

Reproduced with the kind permission of Charles Barker, PrimeMover Associates.
All rights reserved.

However, the good news is that, to a large extent, you already know how to deal with this situation. As learned in the Communications section, rather than getting angry and falling into the downward spiral that we talked about above – where your Consistency will likely be severely challenged – you can adopt a frame of mind for understanding, and start listening actively for the purpose of understanding (not just to get ready to defend or tell them why they're wrong!).

When you find yourself in a situation where you and another person have differing views that can't be explained by your respective interests, consider that you may simply have different perceptions. Neither of you is necessarily right or wrong. You have just reached different conclusions based on your respective ladders of inference.

The same approach we discussed in the Communications section also applies here. Seek to understand and show understanding before seeking to be understood. Acknowledge the other person's perspective (even if you don't agree) so that they feel heard.

Finally, don't hesitate to use the Ladder of Inference openly. Ask the other person to walk you through their thought process step by step, helping you understand how they arrived at their conclusion. Likewise, guide them through your own reasoning to give them a clearer view of your perspective.

Explicitly using the Ladder of Inference can be very beneficial to the relationship. As a general rule, people don't like being exposed to views that contradict their own. This causes cognitive dissonance and can easily feel like these contradictory views are a challenge to them personally, causing them to react either very defensively or with hostility.

By following a logical process and objectively examining different perspectives, the Ladder of Inference helps remove emotion and ego from the discussion. If you're unsure how to introduce it, you might say, "That's an interesting perspective. I'd like to share an alternative one and walk you through how I arrived at it. You can also walk me through your thought process so that I may understand how you reached yours."

Running Effective Meetings

In the final section of this chapter, I'd like to look at how you can run effective meetings.

Few things are more frustrating than sitting in a meeting, wondering why you're there, why so many others are there or what the meeting is even for. This was especially true during the COVID-19 lockdowns when remote work became the norm. Suddenly, middle managers who were no longer in the office had to find new ways to appear busy and justify their roles. The solution? Filling their calendars with online meetings, often serving little purpose beyond demonstrating their "busyness," with as many attendees as possible to make them seem important. In my experience, countless hours were – and still are – wasted this way.

If you can consistently run meetings efficiently and effectively, whether in person or online, and help others do the same, your focus and discipline won't go unnoticed. Those who value their time will certainly appreciate it!

There are four key elements to running effective meetings, known as the 4Ps: purpose(s), process, people and product(s). You can also extend this to 6Ps, if you want to include pastries and pee breaks.

Purpose(s). Hopefully, it is obvious that to be useful and effective, a meeting must have a purpose, possibly more than one. Everyone attending should be aware of and be prepared for it. Examples of purpose would include negotiating a contract to reach points of agreement or any of the topics shown in the illustration below. Any changes or additions to the purpose(s) should not happen on the fly but should be agreed upon by everyone in accordance with the process.

Process. This is probably the most overlooked aspect of any meeting. How is it going to be run? Too often, it's either improvised in the moment ("What's the agenda?" or "How do we make a decision?") or only recognised as an issue after the fact ("Was anyone taking minutes last time?"). The illustration below outlines key process elements to consider.

People. All meetings require the *right* people to be there to achieve the main purpose, but very few require the presence of someone who has nothing to add or input. Make sure that all are identified and invited, and their attendance confirmed in advance. If an essential person is not there, it is highly unlikely that the main purpose(s) will be completely achieved, meaning further calls, meetings and disruption for the attendees.

Product(s). Closely tied to Process, this element entails that everyone should be clear on the expected output or product(s) and who is responsible for delivering them. This could range from meeting minutes (increasingly handled by AI notetakers for online meetings) to draft or final agreements, lists of open points, next steps or action items.

The 4Ps are summarised in the following table:

Running Effective Meetings: the 4Ps

Purpose(s)	Process	People	Product(s)
• Information Exchange	• Provide/Agree agenda in advance	• Are all the right people invited and attending to achieve the purpose and deliver the Product(s)	• Minutes
• Inventing	• Assign roles if necessary (eg chairperson, facilitator, timekeeper, minute taker)		• Action list
• Consultation/ Advice			• Heads of Agreement
• Planning		• Decision makers?	
• Decision	• Separate Inventing from deciding	• Information holders?	• Next Steps
	• Record Ideas in plain view	• Experts?	
	• Avoid unhelpful patterns eg toxic behaviours		

Reproduced with the kind permission of Charles Barker, PrimeMover Associates.

All rights reserved.

NLP

In the Consistency phase, you can use the same NLP process as in the Development and Improvement phases to "switch on" a positive state. This helps reinforce your resilience and consistency. As before, you can adjust all the submodalities to find what "recipe" gives you the best results.

Hypnosis and Hypnotherapy

You will find the link to the hypnotherapy session for the Consistency phase of the ASDIC Framework below.

In this session, I spend more time focusing on the future state and mindset for the resilience and ego-strengthening that you want, in order to help you stay strong and resilient even in the face of difficulties that would have previously thrown you off.

As with all the hypnosis sessions, before you go into the session, I want to be clear that your safety is my first priority, so please read Appendix 2 carefully before using the code to access the hypnotherapy session.

Ok, assuming that you have read Appendix 2 and are ready to go, sit down, ideally with your head and neck supported, or lie down, and scan the code to the hypnosis audio for the Improvement phase.

As with the audio for the Improvement phase, just keep listening to the Consistency session daily until you feel ready to move on. Please also revisit the audios from previous phases whenever you need reinforcement of the attributes from these phases.

Dealing With Anxiety

This chapter's technique for dealing with anxiety is very simple and effective: It involves actively using your peripheral vision to expand your field of focus. By doing that with your eyes, you will also expand your internal field of focus and awareness, helping it move on from its intense focus on your feeling of anxiety.

This technique can be used almost anytime and almost anywhere. Start by picking a specific spot; the easiest would be a spot on the wall in front of you, ideally slightly above your eye line. Keep your vision focused on that one spot. Then, slowly, and moving your eyes as little as possible, expand your field of vision outwards – both side to side and up and down. This will likely feel a bit strange at first as we do not normally consciously activate our peripheral vision.

However, stick at it, and you will soon begin to feel calmer as your focus moves away from the feelings of anxiety.

Chapter Recap

There are two main elements to maintaining consistency in your new approaches. The first is to keep practising and following the new ways (perhaps by setting goals) even when it feels easier not to. The second is to develop approaches and resilience that allow you to deal with people or events that might throw you off balance and revert to the (relative) comfort of what you have always done.

While it is up to you to keep practising, we also looked at techniques you can use to help you deal with the situation that most commonly throws people off course: dealing with difficult people.

We reminded ourselves that the only person you can control is you, and you can't make a difficult person change. But you can create an environment in which they could change and give them the opportunity to do so.

We revisited the concepts from Chapter 7 of actively putting yourself in the other person's shoes, listening actively for understanding (rather than criticising) and letting the other person know you understand what they are saying – even if you don't agree with it – so they feel heard. We layered on the exercise of examining how your own behaviour may be contributing to the difficult relationship.

We dipped a toe into the world of negotiations, and looked at the concepts of "interests" and the "Ladder of Inference" that can be used to help understand why a person may have the view they are putting forward – the one that makes them seem difficult – and help avoid a negative cycle of animosity.

Finally, we looked at the 4Ps of running effective (and efficient) meetings: purpose(s), process, people and product(s).

As you leave this chapter and prepare to move into the world of negotiation in the next, make sure you understand two things: First, the concept of interests and how they differ from positions – and start applying these concepts to analyse difficult conversations. Second, how the Ladder of Inference can lead two people to draw different conclusions from the same data, without either of them necessarily being wrong.

Chapter 9: Bonus Chapter Introduction to Negotiation

"The best general is the one who never fights."
– Sun Tzu

In Chapter 8, I touched on a couple of elements from the world of negotiations, so I thought it worthwhile to include a quick overview of the key elements of just about every negotiation and how to navigate them.

For most people, the word negotiation brings to mind high-powered executives or politicians flanked by an army of lawyers in a (traditionally smoke-filled) boardroom, locked in a battle of wills. They picture intense standoffs – staring contests, fist-banging, shouting – with each side trying to strong-arm or outmanoeuvre the other into surrendering to their demands, whether in a business deal, trade agreement or even a peace treaty.

With that image indelibly seared in most people's subconscious, it is little wonder that even the thought of "a negotiation" stirs the "fight" or, more commonly, "flight" response. As we have discussed, when your subconscious mind detects something it perceives as a danger, or at least something to be avoided, it swings into action and looks to protect you.

However, as we saw in Chapter 8, I believe the word negotiation is best defined as "communication for the purpose of influence." We all negotiate every day in just about every conversation! It is, therefore, not something to be feared, particularly if you understand the basics of what is going on.

Sure, the concept extends right up to multi-billion pound or dollar business contracts and international trade deals and treaties, where the stakes may be higher, but the fundamental premise is still the same: One party wants to reach an agreement with another one or more parties to do something that the first party wants, ideally at as little cost as possible to them.

The "Traditional" Approach to Negotiation

The "fear" factor that many people have in relation to negotiations is based to a large extent on what has come to be regarded as the "traditional" approach, as referenced in the scenes mentioned earlier. This is very much based on one party trying to "reach an agreement" by overpowering the other party.

At the start of our courses on negotiation – generally with executives with some responsibility for business development or sales – we always ask the participants what their aim is in a negotiation. The answers are almost always along the same lines: "Win," "Destroy them," "Get the highest price," "Get the most concessions," or a personal favourite, "Squeeze them until the pips squeak."

Occasionally, people will say: "Stay above our bottom line," "Don't lose" or "Avoid confrontation."

For people who think like that, the negotiation process can be illustrated very much like this:

Classic Positional Bargaining

Opening Offer (extreme position)
Fallback Offer
Last Offer
"Or Else .. !"
Final Offer
Zone of Possible Agreement
Final Offer
Last Offer
"Or Else .. !"
Fallback Offer
Opening Offer (extreme position)

Reproduced with the kind permission of Charles Barker, PrimeMover Associates. All rights reserved.

Does this ring any bells? It represents what we call traditional "positional" negotiation, where each side has its "position" and tries to stick to it at all costs.

Each party enters the discussion expecting confrontation, projecting its worst fears about negotiation onto the other side. Assuming the other party will do the same, it often begins with an extreme position. When it sees the other side doing likewise, it takes this as confirmation that its fears were justified.

So each party expects that the other will behave outrageously, dishonestly, aggressively – choose your own adjective; we've all been there! They then actively look for behaviour to confirm their view. And when they do "see" it, all thanks to confirmation bias, they say, "Aha! We were right to expect the worst," and escalate their own hardball tactics in response. And so, a vicious cycle of mistrust and bad behaviour takes hold.

In this cycle, positions become extreme, individuals grow stubborn and they often dig into stances they don't fully agree with. Concessions are minimal and slow, while behaviours can quickly turn threatening or manipulative. Cue the classic line: "That's my final offer. Take it or leave it." In the end, the so-called resolution is often just splitting the difference between two completely arbitrary numbers.

In this process, a disagreement over positions escalates into a battle of wills and, eventually, a clash of egos. People become personally invested in their stance – even if they weren't fully committed to it at the start – making it increasingly difficult for anyone to back down. The fear of appearing weak keeps both sides stuck, and constructive dialogue falls by the wayside as each party shifts to a "present and defend" mindset.

It becomes exponentially worse when only one party needs to say "no" to prevent agreement – just look at any negotiation between a trade union, an employer and the government.

The alternative to this attack and counterattack approach is to give in to the other party – maybe because the negotiator feels frightened or pressured, maybe because the negotiator thinks it will be "good for the relationship" or maybe because the negotiator just wants a quiet life: "Maybe if I give him what he wants he won't be so nasty to me." That is a false hope. Their nasty behaviour has been rewarded, so they know what to do next time they want something. What people who take this approach also don't realise is that it is ok to say "no" in case it kills the deal. In fact, that is often when constructive dialogue starts.

I believe that everyone should aspire to be better than a positional negotiator. They need to get beyond the "win/lose" mentality that comes from position-based negotiating and aim to think of it as a challenge to collaborate rather than a challenge to be combative. The goal should be to change their thinking from "How do I beat this person?" to "How do I work with this person to solve this problem and get an agreement that is great for both of us?"

To begin with, the position-based approach relies on several assumptions that should be challenged. It assumes that the parties' interests are entirely opposed, that only quantifiable factors matter and that the negotiation is a zero-sum game with a fixed pie. It also fosters mistrust by encouraging the belief that the worst interpretation of the other party's actions is likely correct and that our fears about their intentions must be true.

A Different Way of Thinking: The 5 Elements

We now return to the concept of the Interests-Based Approach, as introduced in Chapter 8. Building on those ideas, we explore a far more effective way to negotiate: interest-based negotiation, also known as collaborative negotiation.

Interest-based negotiation tries to make negotiation a task of jointly finding a solution that works well for all parties, a "win-win" solution. It can be seen as hard on the problem and hard on the process but easy on the people. It is much more collaborative and less a battle of wills and egos.

At first glance, this approach can be seen as a weakness, but it is quite the reverse. It is about being rock-solid behind your interests but flexible in how you satisfy them.

In every negotiation, there are five process elements and a number of softer, interpersonal elements at play. These are easily overlooked and subjugated to the "win-lose" mentality of a positions-based negotiation, to the detriment of all concerned. Interest-based negotiation works with these elements.

These elements will be in every negotiation, whether you choose to pay attention to them or not. How the dials are set on each will vary from case to case. Some will be much more relevant in business negotiations than in a discussion about taking the bins out!. But they will be there. They can be used in a number of ways: as a framework for the negotiation process; as a preparation framework when preparing to negotiate (even if you have very little time); and as a diagnosis tool if negotiations aren't going well (it can help you find choices when there don't appear to be any).

The five process elements are interests, options, alternatives, legitimacy and commitment. The softer elements are around the parties' relationship, rapport, trust and communication, which we have already discussed. Here, we look at each of the process elements.

Interests

Understanding this concept is key to understanding interest-based negotiation, so if you need to refresh your memory, please go back to Chapter 8 before continuing.

It is great to understand the interests of all concerned, but for them to be of any value, you have to do something with them, to make them the basis of the best solution available to you. To do that, you need to invent as many options as possible.

Options

In positional negotiation, the parties tend to go into the discussion with the outcome they want set firmly in their mind and are determined to stick to or get as close to it as possible. They start with an extreme version of it – their "opening position." They present and defend that position and make little or no effort to discover what the other party wants or sees as a problem.

This approach overlooks the fact that there is almost always a range of potential solutions that both sides might find acceptable in meeting their interests.

The goal of interests-based negotiation is to use the parties' understanding of all relevant interests to develop – as collaboratively as possible – as many options as they can to meet the maximum number of interests to the greatest extent. From these options, they can construct a solution that maximises the outcome for both parties.

To do this effectively, you need to separate the process of inventing options from deciding on options, a distinction that can be challenging but is crucial to introduce early. Surprisingly, this approach can even strengthen relationships.

A few years ago, I was involved in negotiating a large IT contract with a major international company. Their lead negotiator, known for his tough, positional style, walked into our first meeting, locked eyes with us, and said, "I want your best people delivering the highest service levels at the lowest price you've ever given." The tension in the room was palpable.

I met his gaze and replied, "That's certainly an option…but I'm sure we can come up with better ones – ones that allow us to work together rather than constantly distrusting and fighting each other." He laughed; the ice was broken, and just a few weeks later, we held an offsite meeting where both our technical and commercial teams sat together, brainstorming options to collaborate and maximise value for both sides.

Inventing options is about finding things you could do, not necessarily things that you will do. The aim is to produce as many as possible and then narrow it down. You may well come up with an option you would not be prepared to live with. The options that you develop may be solutions in their own right or part of a wider package.

It is very easy to fall into the trap of reaching a "solution" before you have explored all possible options. This is suboptimal. Dwelling on a single solution, or taking the first one that comes along that both parties can say yes to because it eases the pain, often leaves money on the table.

When you can get the other party engaged in the process of inventing options with you, a whole new world of possibilities opens up. Most people don't see inventing as part of the negotiating process. So if you can set and observe certain ground rules, your relationship will deepen and the possibilities for mutual benefit will multiply as you brainstorm options.

We have found the following ground rules to be vital:

Separate inventing from deciding. Be clear that you are separating the process of inventing from deciding.

No commitment. No one is committing to anything that is discussed.

No criticism. There is to be no criticism of anything put forward. Silence the voice that says, "That won't work." Critical evaluation comes later.

Encourage thinking outside the box. Even if an idea doesn't work, it may inspire one that does. Focus on generating a wide range of possibilities first and save evaluation for later. Following the communication approach from Chapter 7, use open-ended questions that minimise resistance, such as "What if...?," "Could we...?," "What would be wrong with...?," "What other ideas can we explore...?" and "How can we work together to make this better for everyone?"

Clearly this may all be compressed in an informal or semi-formal discussion, but following the principles will help keep you on track, and help your relationship with the "difficult" person.

Only once you have finished inventing options do you move on to deciding which ones to pursue and then work out which of these can be implemented and on what terms.

We have so far understood interests, we have developed options and chosen the best of them. It can now be tempting to say, "Hey, we have got something here. Let's do this deal." Before that, you need to test that they are fair. In other words, test their legitimacy.

Legitimacy

Almost every negotiator's biggest fear is being cheated or treated unfairly. "Legitimacy" is the way of testing the fairness of a potential agreement by reference to external, objective standards.

Agreements based on objective standards are easier for each side to accept because there is no sense of backing down or being weak. They wield great persuasive power when proposing an agreement to the other side. An agreement based on objective standards is also easier to explain and justify to constituents and critics. It can be presented to them as a deal based on an external benchmark rather than something you came up with yourself.

Objective standards can serve as both a sword and a shield in negotiations. When presenting a proposed outcome, these standards help demonstrate that it is fair and reasonable. At the same time, they can protect you from arbitrary or unreasonable demands. If the other party insists on something without clear justification, it is reasonable to ask, "Where did that number come from?" or "Why do you think that number is fair?" Then require objective evidence to support their position. Standing firm on fairness, backed by objective standards, is far more effective than simply being stubborn.

If the other party produces relevant and acceptable objective criteria, this allows you to back down gracefully, deferring to what seems fair rather than being seen as giving in.

When you think about it, we do this regularly in our personal lives. If you were looking to buy a house, you would research what similar homes in the same neighbourhood had sold for. If you were looking to buy or sell a car, you would check valuation sites for the same make and model.

In many cases, multiple sources of objective criteria exist. While this may seem daunting, it actually provides a range within which a fair solution can be found. The logical approach is to identify the source that best matches your situation and ideally aligns with your interests. But discussing which standards are most relevant is often easier and more productive. This approach also carries more legitimacy than simply arguing over which of two arbitrary positions should prevail.

While I very rarely advocate "splitting the difference" as the way to resolve an impasse, it is much easier to justify the use of this between two positions that can be externally verified as valid, rather than two random arbitrary positions – as positional negotiators are wont to do.

A tip: If you are presenting, say, a price or a desired salary, it is much more effective if you can explain the source of its legitimacy before you give the number. If you start with the number, the other person may well interpret it as a position and will not be listening (but getting ready to attack it) when you get around to explaining why it is fair.

Legitimacy can be a hard element to pin down in an "everyday" discussion with a difficult person, but that should not put you off trying your best to find some standard (even if it is along the lines of, "But you gave Susan two weeks to do a similar project"). If you have one, it is very persuasive and difficult to argue against.

We have now understood interests, developed options and chosen the best of them, and checked that it is an outcome that would have legitimacy. Surely it's now time to do the deal? No, not quite. First you need to check and see if you are making the wisest choice.

Alternatives

It surprises many people to realise that the purpose of negotiation is not always to reach an agreement. The purpose of negotiation is to give you the opportunity to make the best possible choice as to how to meet your interests.

What do I mean by that?

Well, the negotiation is about what you can agree with the other party in order to meet your interests. But there will be other ways, outside of agreement with the other party, in which you can meet your interests. Alternatives is the term that we use for those other ways. They will not always be good, but they will always exist.

Before finalising any negotiation, compare the outcome you've negotiated with the best possible outcome from your alternatives. Choose the outcome that best serves your interests before making a commitment.

Amongst negotiators, the alternative that best meets (or comes closest to meeting) your interests is known as your Best Alternative to Negotiated Agreement (BATNA). This phrase was first used by Fisher and Ury in *Getting to Yes*, and is now widely adopted as part of the *lingua franca* of negotiation.

It can be easy to confuse options and alternatives. A good way to think about it is that Options are potential outcomes that are On the table with the other party (both begin with O), while Alternatives are outcomes that you can generate Away from the table and the other party (both begin with A). Be very careful in using the correct terminology; it is very easy to inadvertently call an alternative an option or vice versa.

There is also often some confusion between the notion of your BATNA and the notion of your "bottom line." They are not the same thing.

In a price negotiation, for example, the seller's bottom line is usually the lowest price they can afford to charge before making a loss (or an unacceptable margin). In the case of the buyer, it is the highest price that they are prepared to pay, perhaps given their financial situation, their budget or just because that's what management told them! It is usually something set by internal considerations.

Your best Alternative or BATNA is different. Your BATNA is what you could do realistically if you walked away from the negotiation with no agreement. It is what you will do on your own if no agreement is reached.

If you have a clear understanding of what you'll do if you walk away from a negotiation, any deal you accept will be a success – meaning it will be better than your best alternative. If it isn't, you shouldn't take it.

Your BATNA is where your greatest leverage lies, yet it is often overlooked or given minimal attention until it seems that talks are going to break down. If you go in knowing exactly what you will do if things fall through, you are in a great position. If your BATNA is good, you can be fearless; if it is bad, you are forearmed.

You always have a BATNA. As said above, it may not be good. It may even be terrible – but you will always have one. You should never walk into a negotiation without knowing what it is. It can be an incredible source of power in any deal-making situation.

As you prepare, be ruthless in analysing your alternatives to determine which one is the best. It is a common mistake to aggregate the cumulative benefit of all your alternatives in your head, which can make you feel that you are in a stronger position than you actually are. You need to focus on each one individually. Think about how you could boost your BATNA. Even as the negotiations progress, constantly be thinking about how you could improve your BATNA, and do it as necessary.

Once you know what it is, ask yourself: Should I negotiate at all? It is ok not to do a bad deal.

After that, analyse the other side's alternatives and assess what you believe to be their BATNA. They will have one too, and it could be a source of great leverage for them. If it is poor, it can be a source of great leverage to you.

Once you believe you have it, think about ways in which you can (legally) weaken it. As negotiations progress, constantly think about how you could weaken the other side's BATNA, and do it as necessary.

If you have a strong BATNA, there is no harm in making the other party aware of it. Be aware of falling into the positional trap of making it a threat – "Do what I want or else" or "I will hurt you because I can." Instead, just explain how it meets your interests better, so it is understood as a logical position.

So now, we have understood interests, developed options and chosen the best of them, checked that it is an outcome that would have legitimacy and that the proposed deal meets our interests better than our BATNA. It's time to capture the value before it disappears. It's time to commit!

Commitment

The last stage of the negotiation process is commitment: committing to the deal in a verbal or written contract.

The first rule of commitment is not to commit to anything until you commit to everything. It is not an uncommon approach – and can seem reasonable – for the other party to suggest that you reach an agreement on, and commit to, main points one at a time. This can work, but often, at the last stage, when you have reached the really tricky, contentious issues, you will find that you have been "salami sliced" and lost the ability to create options that help meet your interests. You have already given away all of your bargaining levers in those early commitments.

That is not to say you can't develop agreements in principle as you go along. Indeed, that can be a good and positive thing. But only commit fully once all points have been agreed upon in a way that meets your interests better than your BATNA.

I won't address how the commitment is documented, but however it is done, some components are key. Lawyers have written tomes on what a good contract should contain, and I'm not going to go down that rabbit hole here! At the very least, just know that any commitment needs to be the following:

Clear. It must be clear what is to be done, who has to do it, how it is established that it is done, how and when they get paid for it and what happens if they don't do it.

Realistic. It must be possible for the parties to do or achieve what they have committed to.

Sufficient. It must cover all aspects that need to be covered for the outcome to be successful.

Operational. It must be capable of being implemented or operationalised, and the parties must have the capacity and resources to do so.

Pulling the Elements Together

Those, then, are the Five Process Elements that are key to maximising the benefits of your negotiations while minimising the personal stress that can come with negotiating.

If you think back to the beginning of this chapter, you will recall the chevron-like representation of the Classic Positional Bargaining process. If we represent the interest-based negotiation process based on these elements and the "softer" interpersonal elements of Rapport, Relationship and Communication, it looks like this:

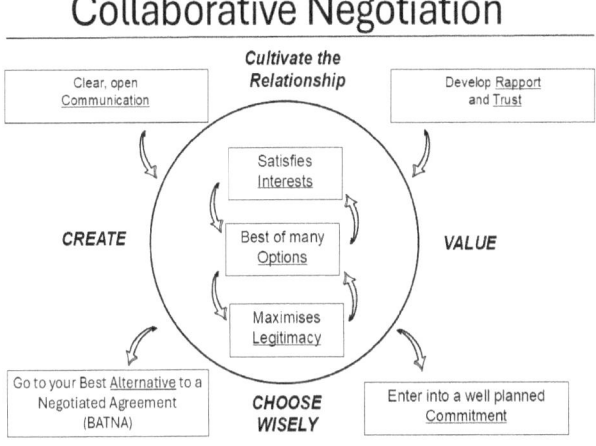

The figure is reproduced, and the term "Collaborative Negotiation" is used with the kind permission of Charles. Barker, PrimeMover Associates. All rights reserved.

I know there are many variations of this diagram, but I prefer this version because I can picture the central circle as the negotiating "table." Here, process elements help address substantive issues, while around the table, rapport and trust are built through communication. Away from the table, each party makes its decisions.

The amazing thing about this approach is this: You want the other person to learn your strategy and follow it! In my experience, if you lead this way, the other side will gladly follow.

Chapter Recap

Most people traditionally think of negotiation as a "win or lose" battle that rewards intransigence and toughness. That approach is known as Positional Negotiation, and most people either adopt an aggressive approach or try to avoid it (or make it as painless as possible).

In many cases, that approach is suboptimal as it is hard on the people involved, focuses on splitting value rather than creating it and often leaves money on the table.

Taking an interests-based approach is more collaborative, easier on the people and can deliver better results.

There are Five Process Elements in interests-based negotiation.

- **Interests.** The underlying reason(s) why you are negotiating in the first place.

- **Options.** Different ways in which Interests can be satisfied.

- **Legitimacy.** Ensuring that agreed options are fair by using external standards.

- **Alternatives.** Ways of achieving a party's interests if there is no agreement.

- **Commitment.** Committing to the agreed solution in a way that is clear, realistic, sufficient and operational.

There are also the softer, interpersonal elements of relationship, rapport, trust and communication.

There are many, many books on the different aspects of negotiation, but you now have a grasp of the key principles behind a successful negotiation.

Chapter 10
Closing Thoughts: Adding Experience & Skill to Knowledge

> *"We are what we repeatedly do.*
> *Excellence, then, is not an act, but a habit."*
> – Will Durant

Congratulations! You have reached the end of the book and your journey through the ASDIC Framework – with a few diversions and side roads thrown in for good measure!

However, as with so many things in life, the end of one journey signifies the beginning of another. Throughout the previous nine chapters, I hope that you have gained knowledge that you did not have before, knowledge that will help you greatly in your quest for success.

The next journey is adding experience and skill to the knowledge. Knowledge without experience is useful, but it is only when you add experience to the mix and see the concepts you have learned play out in real life that you really start to develop. Then you will see your personal growth and change accelerate, and you will start to develop skills in how you use the knowledge, repeating it over and over again until it becomes embedded in your subconscious and just becomes part of you: the way that you act and behave without even thinking about it.

To succeed in any endeavour, I believe that the "holy trinity" of knowledge, experience and skill are required.

What do I mean by "knowledge" and "experience"? Aren't they the same thing? No, absolutely not. If you have read a book on, say, learning how to drive a car, you have the knowledge of how to do it, but until you have sat behind the wheel of that car, you do not have experience of putting that knowledge into practice. Similarly, it is only when you apply your knowledge and put it into practice that you start to develop the skills to use the knowledge effectively, in a way that's right for you.

The next step in your journey is transforming knowledge into experience and skill. While knowledge is valuable on its own, real development happens when you apply it in real-life situations. As you witness these concepts in action, your growth will accelerate, and you'll refine how you use what you've learned. Through repetition, these skills become second nature, deeply embedded in your subconscious, until they shape the way you act and respond instinctively.

The journey moves you from not really being competent in what you are doing but not even knowing that; to being aware that you lack competence; to being aware that you are good at what you do; and ending up with competence being so much a part of you that you no longer need to think about it, as demonstrated in the diagram below.[15]

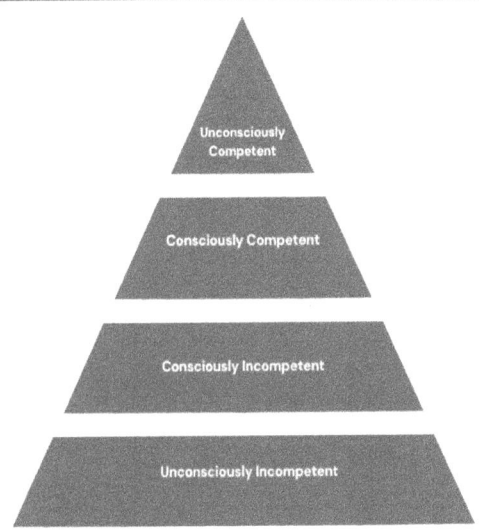

I wish you every success on this journey, in your career and in life!

While most of this will be down to you, I can help. As you have probably gathered, I run corporate and group training courses on developing a "success" mindset, as well as helping clients on a one-to-one basis. I also speak at conferences on these topics. If you are interested in finding out more, you can get in touch with me in the Resources section at the end of the book.

In case you want to learn more, I have also included a list of materials that can help in the Resources section. This is not an exhaustive list, but it includes resources that I have found useful. Like most executives, my pile of "books that I really want to read" and my list of links to "training that I really want to take" are far bigger than the list of the books I have read and training courses I have taken!

Thank you for reading, and good luck on your quest!

Appendix 1: Conditions Matrix

How it presents/ affects interactions	Limiting Beliefs	Impostor Syndrome	Fear of Failure	Fear of Looking Stupid	Comparison With Others	Anxiety	Self-Doubt	The Feeling of Not Belonging	Fear of Public Speaking	Feeling Stuck
Hesitation to take on new challenges	✓									✓
Self-sabotage or procrastination			✓			✓	✓			
Difficulty in setting and achieving ambitious goals	✓		✓				✓			✓
Negative self-talk and doubt about abilities	✓	✓	✓	✓			✓	✓		
Persistent self-doubt		✓	✓				✓	✓		
Overworking to compensate for perceived inadequacies		✓				✓				
Fear of failure and rejection		✓	✓			✓	✓		✓	

How it presents/ affects interactions	Limiting Beliefs	Impostor Syndrome	Fear of Failure	Fear of Looking Stupid	Comparison With Others	Anxiety	Self-Doubt	The Feeling of Not Belonging	Fear of Public Speaking	Feeling Stuck
Avoidance of leadership roles	✓	✓	✓	✓	✓				✓	✓
Reluctance to speak up in meetings				✓		✓			✓	
Avoidance of new or unfamiliar tasks				✓		✓	✓		✓	
Over-preparation or excessive caution				✓					✓	
Seeking constant validation		✓			✓				✓	
Envy and resentment towards colleagues					✓			✓		
Dissatisfaction with personal achievements			✓		✓			✓		
Constant self-evaluation against others' success					✓	✓	✓	✓	✓	

How it presents/affects interactions	Limiting Beliefs	Impostor Syndrome	Fear of Failure	Fear of Looking Stupid	Comparison With Others	Anxiety	Self-Doubt	The Feeling of Not Belonging	Fear of Public Speaking	Feeling Stuck
Negative self-image					✓	✓	✓			
Constant worry and overthinking					✓	✓	✓		✓	
Physical symptoms like sweating, trembling or rapid heartbeat					✓	✓			✓	
Difficulty in concentrating and making decisions					✓	✓				
Hesitant in decision-making	✓	✓	✓	✓			✓			
Reluctance to accept praise or compliments		✓							✓	
Appears disengaged or uncooperative					✓			✓		
Perceived as lacking ambition or drive	✓	✓	✓							

Appendix 2:

Hypnosis Health Warning

Please do not participate in any of the hypnosis sessions in the links or codes in this book if you are under 18 or if any of the following apply to you, unless your doctor has advised you that it is safe:

- You suffer from any form of psychosis
- You are schizophrenic
- You suffer from bipolar disorder
- You suffer from narcolepsy
- You have a heart condition
- You are pregnant
- You are under the care of a mental health practitioner, or under the care of any medical practitioner for any psychological condition
- You are under the influence of drugs or alcohol

While, hopefully, it is self-evident, please do not listen to any of the hypnosis sessions in the links or codes in this book when you are driving or operating machinery.

Resources

You may contact me using the details below.

Websites

Each of these websites contains more information about the services I offer in the relevant fields and how to contact me.

www.donaldhamilton.co.uk

www.donaldhamiltoncoaching.com (this links to www.donaldhamilton.co.uk)

www.donaldhamiltonhypnotherapy.com

You may also email me directly at:
info@donaldhamiltoncoaching.com

Other Websites/Courses

Ali Campbell: www.alicampbell.com

Havening Technique: www.havening.org

Freddy Jaquin: Freddy Jacquin, UK Hypnotherapist: inventor of The Arrow Technique

Anthony Jacquin: www.anthonyjacquin.com

Jacquin Hypnosis Academy: www.jacquinhypnosisacademy.com

PrimeMover Associates: PrimeMover Associates, Inc. - Advice, Mediation & Training

Books

Bandler, Richard and Grinder, John: *Frogs into Princes*. Real People Press, 1979

Bierman, Steve: *Healing - Beyond Pills & Potions*. Gyro Press International, 2020

Campbell, Ali: *NLP Made Easy*. Hay House, 2015

Campbell, Ali: *Just Get on With It* (Revised, Updated Edition). Hay House, 2015

Cialdini, Robert: *Influence: The Psychology of Persuasion*. Harper, 1984

Elman, Dave: *Hypnotherapy*. Westwood Publishing, 1977

Fisher, Roger and Ury, William: *Getting to Yes*. Random House, 1982

Fisher, Roger and Ury, William: *Getting Past No*. Bantam Books, 1991

Stone, Douglas and Patton, Bruce and Heen, Sheila: *Difficult Conversations.* Penguin, 1999

Jacquin, Anthony: *Reality is Plastic.* Anthony Jacquin, 2016

Jacquin, Freddy: *Hypnotherapy: Methods, Techniques and Philosophies.* Freddie H. Jacquin, 2018

Jacquin, Freddy: *The Exquisite Art of Hypnosis and Hypnotherapy.* Jacquin Hypnosis Academy, 2023

Tiers, Marissa: *The Anti-Anxiety Toolkit.* The Center for Integrative Hypnosis, 2011

Tract, Brian: *GOALS!* Berrett- Koehler Publishers Inc, 2003

References

1. Bierman, S., *Healing: Beyond Pills & Potions*, Gyro Press International, 2020.

2. Bandler, R. and Grinder, J., *The History of Magic Part 1: A Book about Language and Therapy*, Palo Alto, California, Science & Behavior Books, 1975.

3. The Havening Techniques, 'What is Havening', *Havening.org*, available at https://www.havening.org/resources/documents/What_is_havening.pdf (accessed December 2024).

4. Tracy, B., *GOALS!: How to Get Everything You Want – Faster Than You Ever Thought Possible*, Oakland, California, Berrett-Koehler Publishers Inc., 2003.

5. 'Inside the Mind of a Master Procrastinator | Tim Urban | TED', *YouTube*, available at https://youtu.be/arj7oStGLkU?si=rcXsksW-NIVIz6YD (accessed July 2024).

6. Twain, M., *Corn Pone Opinions*, in *Europe and Elsewhere*, ed. Albert Bigelow Paine, written in 1901, first published 1923.

7. Bandler, R. and Grinder, J., *Frogs into Princes: Neuro Linguistic Programming*, Moab, Utah, Real People Press, 1979.

8. Cialdini, R., *Influence: The Psychology of Persuasion*, New York, Harper Collins, 2007 (first published 1984).

9. Maister, J., Galford, R. and Green, C., *The Trusted Advisor*, UK, Simon & Schuster UK, repr. edn, 2002 (first published 2001).

10. Martineau, P., *Motivation in Advertising: Motives that Make People Buy*, New York, Toronto and London, McGraw-Hill, 1971 (first published 1957).

This quote is generally attributed to Martineau, but he may have been quoting from an article titled *Is Anybody Listening?* by William H. Whyte published in 1952.

11. Mehrabian, A., *Silent Messages: Implicit Communication of Emotions and Attitudes*, Wadsworth Publishing Company, 1972.

12. Gottman, J., *The Seven Principles for Making Marriage Work*, Harmony Publishing, rev. edn, 2015 (first published 1999).

13. Fisher, R. and Ury, W., *Getting to Yes*, London, Random House, 1999 (first published in the UK in 1982).

14. Ury, W., *Getting Past No: Negotiating in Difficult Situations*, New York, Bantam Dell, 2007 (first published 1991).

15. DePhillips, F. A., Berliner, W. M. and Cribbin, J. J., *Management of Training Programs*, USA, Richard D. Erwin, Inc., 1960.

About the Author

Donald Hamilton was born in Glasgow, Scotland, where he went to school and studied law at Strathclyde University. He moved to London in 1987, where he practised law both at a law firm and for Accenture, a multi-national corporation where he held various Head of Legal roles and executive positions, as well as becoming a member of the faculty at Accenture's Centre of Negotiation Excellence.

During that time, Donald travelled extensively, including living in Chicago for two years, and took a career break teaching water sports in Greece for 9 months in 1993.

On leaving Accenture in 2010, Donald and his wife took their children, then aged 11 and 9, out of school and travelled around the world for nine months, visiting 11 countries.

Inspired to be a storyteller by his father, the 2010 trip gave Donald the opportunity to release his writing talents. His first book, *This is Madness*, contains the journals he and his family wrote on their trip and was published in December 2012. He also has two children's books, *The Boy Who Farted and Flew to the Moon* and *The Boy Who Farted and Landed on Mars*, under the pen name "Ivan Offolbot" (think about it!). All these books are available on Kindle.

On his return, Donald followed a more entrepreneurial lifestyle. He ran a consultancy specialising in negotiation and a small property business and began his journey as a writer and publisher. He also worked as a standup comedian, performing in the UK and US.

He set up his own negotiation consultancy in 2010 before joining Hewlett Packard as a strategic negotiator, moving on to become a commercial director at its spin-offs, Hewlett Packard Enterprise and DXC Technology.

After leaving DXC, he retrained as a clinical hypnotherapist and NLP practitioner before returning to his entrepreneurial journey. Donald established his hypnotherapy, NLP and executive training and coaching practices while also maintaining a small legal and commercial consulting practice.

Donald lives in Surrey with his wife and, from time to time, one or both of their adult children.

www.ingramcontent.com/pod-product-compliance
Lightning Source LLC
Chambersburg PA
CBHW050340010526
44119CB00049B/633